NAKED AND UNAFRAID

NAKED AND UNAFRAID

5 Keys to Abandon Smallness,
Overcome Criticism, and Be All You
Are Meant to Be

KEVIN GERALD

Nashville   New York

This book is dedicated to my grandsons, Kyan and Kody, who inspire me to fight for our future. I love you to the moon and back.

CONTENTS

RISK EXPOSURE

"Avoiding danger in the long run is no safer than outright exposure. Life is either a daring adventure or nothing."

—Helen Keller

"Never let the fear of striking out keep you from playing the game."

—Babe Ruth

CHAPTER 1

WINDOW VERSUS STREET

It was a day unlike any other day in history. For his entire life, David had dreamed of a time when the highly revered national artifact known as the Ark of the Covenant would be brought back to a place of prominence in the now prosperous city of Jerusalem.

As the symbol of God's presence in the nation, the Ark had been present since the days of Moses. David's ancestors had carried the Ark across deserts and onto battlefields and had recovered it from enemies who stole it. For the past eighty years, they had kept it in private estates out of the public eye.

Since not everyone knew where the Ark was, it had been forgotten by many. But not by David, who was now king. Like a creative architect, he had envisioned this day for years—the day he would bring the Ark to the city where it belonged and, in doing so, would give the people something to celebrate and the God of their fathers the glory He deserved.

This was one of the major milestones preparing the way for David to build God a house that would be of "great magnificence and fame" (1 Chron. 22:5), which explains why thousands of people left their shops and homes and filled the streets of Jerusalem, hoping to get a glimpse of history past and be part of history present.

To say it was festive would be an understatement. Especially when the king himself broke royal protocol by taking off his royal robes, wrapping his linen garments up around his waist, and heading out into the streets.

The streets were not where the king was *expected* to be.

Then the music in him met the music around him. He started dancing with those who danced and celebrated alongside the working-class people. He was unreserved in his joy and unrestrained in his celebration. Had there been a camera, its photo would have accompanied the cover story of every major news outlet in the world, along with the headline "A Disrobed King Dances in the Streets."

David had just had one of his best days. A personal mission was now accomplished, a milestone had been reached, and a dream had come true. After David danced in the streets celebrating the return of the Ark of the Covenant to Jerusalem, the party ended at the front lawn of the palace. Scripture says he returned to bless his household.

Had there been paparazzi, a journalist, or a news opinion columnist present, there would have also been another story biting at the heels of those headlines like a hostile takeover. This story would have a different twist. Instead of a picture of David dancing in the street, it would include a picture of Michal, David's wife, seated in a window above the street and staring down at David with a look of contempt on her face, offering every journalist in Jerusalem a scathing headline to match the king's.

Before David could enter the palace, Michal, his wife, came rushing out to confront him like a raging fire moving through a dry forest: "How the king of Israel distinguished himself today! He uncovered himself today in the eyes of his servants' maids as one of the foolish ones shamelessly uncovers himself!" (2 Sam. 6:20 NASB).

We don't know if her harsh words began in that moment, or if they built into an eruption when David returned home later that evening. What we do know is that David did not measure up to Michal's idea of what the proper protocol for a king should be, and she let him know it. She had no problem calling him a fool whose behavior dishonored her, the royal family, and the people of the nation.

When you read the Scripture, you might conclude that David's wife was mad at him because he took off his clothes and danced in the streets. In reality, it wasn't about that. David was physically clothed. Michal was angry because David had taken off the royal robes that were protocol for a king to wear in public. Evidently, he wanted to have a good time singing and dancing in the streets, but the royal robe was too stuffy, too formal. So David removed his garments so that he could join in the party. To Michal, it was ridiculous. It was careless. It was overexposure. For David to be in the streets, vulnerable, expressive, interactive, felt dangerous, even reckless to her.

Before we jump to the conclusion that Michal was just a crazy unreasonable woman, let's remember that we've all spent some time in the window. Uncomfortable with going to the street, we've all made the choice to keep our distance, play it safe, and watch from the window.

Window watching has its own "window logic": it provides a reasonable argument that says the window is the best, safest position to be in. It is always based on some form of fear that causes people to pull away from participation.

This was the case for Michal. The fact that Michal was angry and afraid can, at least in part, be explained by the way she was raised. Her father, King Saul, went from being a fearless leader to becoming insecure and suspicious of everyone around him. By the time David came on the scene, Saul was a paranoid monarch who kept his guard up and kingly status in place 24/7.

In the early days of David's teenage life in the palace, Saul was so miserable and troubled that he would send for David to play music to help him relax and find peace of mind. When David played the harp, it served as a sedative to the fears that were driving Saul into a deeper, darker place of seclusion.

Window logic tells us that it's not safe to get close to people, to interact with people, or to connect with people. It tells us that we're more likely to get hurt or be taken advantage of if we engage. So, the better plan—the safer course of action—always seems to be to pull back and keep your distance from people.

Naturally, those types of beliefs are easily transferred from a strong father to his children, and this appeared to be the case with Saul and Michal. Saul's window logic seemed to be the source of Michal's own ideas about proper protocol for a king. In her mind, the window was the right place for her, and if David was going to be in the streets physically, he needed to at least stay in the window emotionally. That's what window logic says:

Wave, but don't shake hands.

Smile, but don't trust anyone.

Look relaxed, but don't let your guard down.

Talk, but don't embrace.

Follow the rules, stay on guard, keep your distance.

Stay in the window.

Although Michal had become David's wife and David was now the king, her view of life was still influenced by her father. If that's what you're raised with, then you've heard all the logic and bought into the idea that kings don't dance in the streets. Smart people, especially kings, keep their distance and follow proper protocol, which means they stay in the window.

I get it. Window logic is rational, sensible, and easy to defend. It keeps you from being too vulnerable.

> Window logic tells us that it's not safe to get close to people, to interact with people, or to connect with people.

In fact, I'm guessing that many of you are like me in the sense that you've heard people talk about vulnerability as a good thing, and in your mind, you wrestled with what that looked like. What does it mean to be vulnerable? Because the very word *vulnerable* feels as if you're putting yourself in a position of weakness. An unsafe position. A position to be taken advantage of. To leave the window and go to the streets doesn't seem like a good idea. It feels like overexposure, even dangerous sometimes.

Which is why I questioned a few members of our message research team at my church when they recommended that I preach a series on vulnerability. I had asked them to help me by researching the most common felt needs of people and was surprised when they came back with data supporting their recommendation. The data showed that while people agree that vulnerability is essential, they feel completely overwhelmed by the thought of it. Perhaps that's because of where our thoughts go when we hear the word *vulnerability*.

So, before I let you get too far into speculation and possibly decide that this book is not for you, let me say this:

Vulnerability is not weakness.

It doesn't mean setting aside common sense.

It doesn't mean getting naked with everyone.

It doesn't mean committing yourself to everyone.

It doesn't mean trusting everyone.

It doesn't mean listening to everyone.

It doesn't mean giving everyone the keys to your house.

Now that we have that out of the way, let me also say that vulnerability doesn't support a "looking out for yourself" approach to life. It's the opposite of playing it safe. It's counterintuitive and can be dangerous, difficult, and risky. Vulnerability is making a move with no guarantee of the outcome.

In the spirit of full disclosure, every personality test I've ever taken shows that I have high levels of resistance when it comes to trusting other people, and my greatest fear is the fear of being taken advantage of. For those who are interested, on a DiSC assessment, I'm a Di, and on an Enneagram assessment, an 8. If you're familiar with these tests, you now know my issues and why I'm the least likely to see vulnerability as anything other than weakness.

> **Vulnerability is making a move with no guarantee of the outcome.**

When my wife, Sheila, and I first met, I said, "Hello." She extended her hand and said, "Hi, I'm Sheila, and I'm shy." Which is absolutely not true! I shook her hand and said, "I'm Kevin, and I'm careful." Evidently that wasn't true either, because a year later we were married!

Like all relationships, ours began with a game, the game of "my terms, my time." It goes like this: "I'll let you know the real me on my terms, at my time. Until then, you will know a version of me."

We begin relationships like that because it's reasonable. It's not smart to open your life equally to everyone. Different relationships should have varying degrees of openness.

The problem comes when we get stuck in the window but we still expect to experience the relational growth that can only happen when we drop our guard, stop protecting ourselves, and do life in an open, walls-down way. Relationships won't get better by staying in the window; they only get better in the street. Marriages, friendships, families get stronger in the place where people interact, mingle, engage, and yes, become vulnerable.

There's a little animal you've probably heard of called the hedgehog. On a cold day, a hedgehog will search out other hedgehogs to huddle up with to keep warm. But because of his prickly spines he is forced to make a choice: get close, get stabbed, and stay warm, or keep away, stay safe, and freeze.

Which is exactly how we feel after relational experiences that bring us pain. Should I get close and stay warm where I will also be vulnerable to getting hurt? Or should I stay away, stay safe, but probably freeze? This is window logic versus street logic—stay away and freeze (window logic) or get close, be warm, and risk pain (street logic).

Everything about us gets stronger when we live with vulnerability, openness, and confidence. There's a freedom we gain when we drop our guard and engage life with certainty. Vulnerability is defined as the quality or state of being exposed to the possibility of being attacked or harmed. Simply put, it's openness that exposes your thoughts, ideas, effort, work, and/or leadership, all while knowing that others might criticize and judge you for it. It's a willingness to absorb the disapproval of others and learn from it versus being held back from the progress you are called to in your own life.

This book is about a decision we all face. A decision we make repeatedly, often without even knowing it. This decision positions us in one of two places. And it not only influences but also ultimately determines our life experience. We can either watch from the window or dance with abandon in the streets.

Study Questions

1. After reading this chapter, what does "staying in the window" and "dancing in the streets" mean to you?
2. When was the last time you experienced someone showing vulnerability in a way that inspired you?
3. Is your tendency by nature to stay in the window or dance in the streets?
4. Vulnerability is defined in this book as "making a move with no guarantee of the outcome." Think about a time you were vulnerable. Was it easy or hard for you to make a move with no guarantee of the outcome?
5. What do vulnerability and courage look and sound like for you after reading this chapter? How has your perspective changed?

CHAPTER 2

THE RISK OF EXPOSURE

I'm writing just the first section of this book, and I'm wondering if I'm going to be able to get it right. For now, since I'm the only one looking at these sentences, I'm able to hit the keyboard with no hesitation, knowing that I can cut, slice, and revise. No one will see the failed attempts to find my flow or get my thoughts together. It feels safe in this space because no one else sees what I'm attempting to do except for me. But for a book, a song, an idea, a dream to have a chance of making a difference in the lives of others, the person executing it has to risk exposure.

Which makes me wonder:

How many ideas are never shared?

How many books never get written and published?

How many companies are never created?

How many potential relationships never get the chance to ignite?

How many creative writers, talented artists, brilliant in-

fluencers, and strong leaders are playing it safe rather than risk the rejection, the criticism, or the failure?

The common denominator of window logic is always fear:

- Fear of stepping out
- Fear of messing up
- Fear of what someone will think or say
- Fear of not measuring up
- Fear of not being good enough or smart enough
- Fear of disappointment
- Fear of rejection

You may wonder what sorts of people put themselves out there. What kinds of people speak to strangers, create companies, start churches, write songs, or chase dreams? Are they people who have no fear? I don't think so. Fear happens to everyone when they start to push past the familiar and risk exposure.

So, if they're not fearless, what are they? They're people who take risks despite the fear they feel. They understand the value of putting themselves out there despite the urge to play it safe. In every pursuit of purpose there comes a time when you have to decide that there is something more important than avoiding risk or steering clear of criticism—something more important than staying safe until you die.

Condoleezza Rice became one of the most powerful women in the history of US government. How did she do it? She grew up in segregated Alabama. Her grandfather was a poor cotton farmer. Her mom and dad were schoolteachers in a segregated school. At a young age, she became a world class ice skater and concert-level pianist. She graduated from high school at the age of fifteen, went on to the University of Denver, and finished with a degree in political science at the age of nineteen.

When somebody asked her how that happened, how could a person go from where she was to where she is now, Rice said, "My parents had me absolutely convinced that you may not be able to have a hamburger at Woolworth's, but you can be President of the United States."[1]

The reason I love this story is that her parents didn't ignore the reality related to their African American history. They acknowledged the prejudice that existed toward their skin color represented by the now famous sit-in that happened in 1960 when four African American college students were denied service at the food counter of a Woolworth store in Greensboro, North Carolina. But in the same sentence they told her to never let that stop her from believing she could be the president of the United States. The wisdom of her parents was in knowing that the only way to push past the negative history was to stay focused on creating new and better realities.

> Fear happens to everyone when they start to push past the familiar and risk exposure.

New and better realities are not created by staying in the window. They are created by putting yourself out there and not letting your past history, your feelings of rejection, the possibility of criticism, or your personal pain keep you from the risk of exposure that goes along with life in the streets.

LEAVING THE WINDOW

At twenty-six years old, I was offered the opportunity to become the pastor of a church. They had started building a structure but were unable to complete it because they had run out of money. The church was located in a suburban area of Seattle-Tacoma, far from where I lived at the time, which meant my wife, Sheila, three-year-old daughter, Jodi, and I had to move 2,600 miles from our home in St. Louis to a place where the only people we knew were the few church members we had met when I had previously been a guest speaker at that church. We borrowed money, maxed out our credit cards, and moved into an eight-hundred-square-foot apartment with used furniture given to us by some families in the church. Needless to say, it wasn't what you would want if you were looking for job security. Prior to that, I may have leaned out the window, but until then I had never left the window to head into the street.

At first, the fear I felt was subtle, the kind of apprehension anyone might feel when you're leaving home, stepping out, and going somewhere new. What I soon discovered was that my greatest fear wasn't fear of moving across the country to the unknown. But rather the comments and criticism of those who had doubts about me as a leader. That's when real fear started to sink into my soul, because I realized that at least some of what they said was true. They said I was young and in over my head...true. They said I didn't know what I was getting myself into...true. They said I had no formal financial education, no degree in business, and had not graduated seminary...true, true, and true.

I had never felt that exposed to critics before—the kind of exposure where you have the urge to hide but nothing to hide behind. It was all due to the fact that I knew that people knew the truth about me: my inability, my lack of experience, and my youthful naïveté.

So now what? Any reasonable person could easily come to the conclusion that a twenty-six-year-old rookie pastor had no business taking on the challenge of a church that was shrinking in size, deep in debt, out of money, and several months behind in their mortgage payments.

At that low point and for a few years after, it seemed to me that the smart people were the ones who stayed in the window, while I was struggling to survive and find some financial stability. Many times, I wondered, *What have I done? What was I thinking to bring my wife and daughter on this crazy journey?* I clearly remember telling myself, *If I ever get in a secure place again, I'll be smart enough to not risk that kind of exposure.*

In the next five years, with substantial church growth and several miracles later, we found ourselves in a place of strength. The mortgage was refinanced, the bills were paid, classroom construction was completed, and our church's attendance had passed the one thousand mark, after starting with fewer than eighty people. Even though we were in a bedroom community, growth continued to the point where we had an architect draw up plans for a new auditorium on our property.

In that season without big problems, I had arrived where I thought I wanted to be. Things had settled down and I had settled in. I had won some battles as a leader, I had the respect of my critics, and even though we were considering taking on a building project, I was determined to minimize the risk. That's where we got stuck. It's where a lot of people get stuck. In the place where you decide to play it safe and not take any risk. The city didn't want us to build another building on our property. Now remember, I had assumed that if I ever got to a safe place like I was in, I would never leave the secure seat in the window again. I had assumed that the window was where smart people were, and that's where I wanted to be.

What surprised me was how restless I became when our path forward was blocked. I started to realize that even if we built a building, the location we were in would limit our ability to be more than a community church.

Sheila said to me one night as I lay in bed staring at the ceiling, "You're going to leave, aren't you?" I played dumb and asked her why she would ask that, while wondering, *How did she know what I was thinking?* She was right (as usual). I was contemplating what our next move could be as a family.

On one hand, it felt good to feel safe. We had entered our thirties and had just built our first house in a small rural area away from everything. We even had a beautiful view of Mount Rainier out our bedroom window. Jodi, my daughter, had started school in a small town close to where we lived, and for the first time in our married life, we were in what felt like a safe and secure place.

But what I thought would be true for me turned out to be just the opposite. It wasn't that I felt ungrateful. I knew that what had happened was not to be taken lightly. But safety and security didn't feel like I had assumed it would feel, which is why I was trying to sort out what I was feeling. I kept telling myself, *This is how smart people live. They work hard to have security and then they play it safe—so don't mess it up!* On the other hand, I was beginning to think my time in the Pacific Northwest was over. Maybe God had a new assignment for me.

Then the unthinkable happened. A church a few miles away with a much larger campus invited me to a new adventure in street life. They not only had the bigger facility we needed but also had a location that would give us a regional presence in Tacoma with easier interstate access south to Olympia and north to Seattle.

However, in many ways it felt like déjà vu. A church had split, a bank had foreclosed on the property, and I was being invited to the dance. The further I got into the conversation, the more exposed and vulnerable I felt. I wanted more time to prepare, to plan, to build up a financial reserve that would minimize the risk. Unfortunately, that kind of time was not an option. The advice people were giving me was mixed. Some people around me were excited. They saw this as an answer to prayer. Others were less comfortable with it and believed it was just too risky, especially since we didn't have time to plan for it. Some moments I felt a groundswell of assurance and faith. At other times I wondered, *What if this doesn't go well? What will we do if it doesn't work?*

NO GUARANTEE

The one thing that all vulnerability has in common is that it never comes with a guarantee. Even something as simple as a smile feels vulnerable because there's no guarantee it will be returned. Someone might ignore us or look the other way, so rather than risk it we hold back the generous gesture. The lack of certainty, no money back, no smile back, no time back, no rewind button is what causes us to hesitate or pass up opportunities. Rather than heading to the street we stay in the window. The vulnerability is too uncomfortable. The higher the guarantee, the less the vulnerability. The lower the guarantee, the greater the vulnerability. So whether it's an honest conversation you dread, a change you want to make, a kindness you want to show, a relationship you're getting involved in, or a business you're starting, where the guarantee ends is where vulnerability begins.

You know what I really wanted? I really wanted God to write a simple "yes" or "no" on my bedroom wall in bright green paint. Like, *C'mon, God, is that really asking too much? Even a Y or an N and I'll get the message!*

> **Even something as simple as a smile feels vulnerable because there's no guarantee it will be returned.**

But when I prayed, I felt like God was saying it was *my* choice. I could embrace it, and He would be with me through the process, or I could pass on it. It wasn't as if I felt like I had to do it, but rather that I had an opportunity to determine the possibilities. Since then, I've realized that that's a predictable pattern in my relationship with God.

We think His will is always between two options, one against the other—option A or B. We toil over it, thinking one is the right choice and the other is the wrong choice. Although that can be true when it comes to how we live our lives, it's not the case when neither option is a wrong choice. More often than not, the will of God is like a circle with two or more options inside the circle.

One example of this in Scripture is when Abram's and Lot's herds had grown to the extent that they needed more space. Abram asked Lot to choose which direction he wanted to go, and Abram said he would be glad to go in the opposite direction. Lot chose the more fertile land, and Abram was fine with that. Abram had heard God say, "All the land that you see I will give to you and your offspring forever" (Gen. 13:15 ESV).

The reason this is important to know is that it can liberate you from the fear of missing God's will. That fear, like all fear, will weaken your ability to make decisions that you are free to make. Knowing that God is with you wherever you go is a powerful part of being vulnerable and strong at the same time—vulnerable enough to risk exposure and strong enough to make decisions in the face of uncertainty and fear.

I accepted the invitation. The dance was not private, but public. It wasn't just a decision I made; many joined me, and together we headed into new territory and embarked on two major challenges at the same time: the merging of two congregations and the decision to take on a debt beyond what seemed possible for us. We were no longer in the window. Our team and the newly formed church family were now on a crazy adventure together. There were no guarantees.

It's funny to talk about, but our theme song at the time was a popular contemporary Christian song with the lyrics "Saddle up your horses, we have a trail to blaze."[2] We would sing it in the car and in the hallways at church and smile at one another.

I often felt anxious, especially on Mondays, when I was waiting for income totals and then going into the weekly Monday night finance meeting to see where we were and what we could do. At that time, Peter Wagner was the recognized expert on church growth. He observed our process and called it the biggest church merger on record.

Looking back, it's evident that God was with us and

blessed us. He opened doors for us. He brought key people to help us. There was tangible evidence of his favor on a weekly basis. It was as if the moment we decided to take a walk on the wild side, God said, "I'm right there with you every step of the way."

Scripture says, "Unless the LORD builds the house, those who build it labor in vain" (Ps. 127:1 NRSV). It doesn't say those who *watch it be built*. We are not called to be bystanders or spectators for what God wants to do in our lives. We are called to build. To persevere. To leave the bleachers and invest ourselves in a lifetime of attempting things that matter more than the risk we take to accomplish them.

When we merged those two churches together, it was without a doubt a watershed event. It was a catalyst that changed the trajectory of our lives, and God used it to change the future of many people. It's the essence of this book and in part why I believe so strongly in putting yourself out there, making yourself vulnerable, and not playing it safe.

When I first came to the Northwest, it was risky, but I had a lot less to lose. This decision, on the other hand, felt like we had a lot more to lose. Even though I was telling people that there was no guarantee that it would work, I knew that people were putting their confidence in me as a leader and that, to a certain extent, my reputation was on the line. At the same time, the high stakes that made it a scary decision also made it a pivotal, memorable, and incredibly rewarding event in the lives of all of us who were a part of that season.

It's human nature to want high rewards with low risk, to want big results with small effort. But that's not the way it works. Every time you see someone who has experienced an unusual level of blessings in their life, you can be sure there was a high price paid in the process.

Maybe you're experiencing the paralysis of analysis right now while trying to make a right decision instead of a wrong one. It could be that neither is wrong, and you need the assurance that God will be with you in whichever decision you make. The further you go in this book, the more I hope to persuade you that street dancing is better than window watching. As Lee Ann Womack famously sang, "I hope you dance."[3]

Study Questions

1. How is your life different when you approach situations with openness and confidence? Can you identify a place where you feel most confident?
2. How can you approach decision-making in your life considering that the will of God is like a circle?
3. What are some fears you are facing in this season of your life? What can you do to move forward despite the fear you may feel?
4. Think about a time you have pushed past fear. What types of feelings went through your mind before, during, and after you faced your fear head-on?

CHAPTER 3

PLAYING IT SAFE
IS DANGEROUS

There are a lot of warnings that discourage us from taking risks but not much is said about the dangers of playing it safe. The dangers we're often warned about are the dangers of taking too much risk. We see headlines that describe the cross-country skier who gets caught in an avalanche or the company that went bankrupt when real estate took a downturn. Yet we never see headlines that read, "Low-Risk Approach Forces Business to File Bankruptcy" or "Divorced Couple Regrets Not Going to Marriage Counseling Because They Were Afraid of What People Might Say" or "Man Retires after Mediocre Career and Wishes He Would Have Taken More Risks." It's not that these things don't happen. They happen all the time. It's just that it's not talked about as much.

Maybe you've reflected back on how people have treated you in the past and felt wiser in your decision to not let people get close to you again. Or perhaps you've learned how to sidestep commitment, keep your conversations superficial, and navigate any attempts people make to include you in a circle of friendship and community. We've all had some if not all of these responses in our attempts to protect ourselves from overexposure and play it safe. The interesting thing is that when people do this, it rarely occurs to them that there are very real dangers in playing it safe. Helen Keller said it like this: "Avoiding danger in the long run is no safer than outright exposure. Life is either a daring adventure or nothing." This logic is counterintuitive to most, if not all, people—most believe that avoiding danger *is safer* than outright exposure. It's not just older or retired people who believe this. Millennials are less likely to become entrepreneurs than any recent generation before them. I'm not saying it's unreasonable that they would want to avoid danger that they associate with taking risk, especially when you consider what they have seen in recessions and mortgage failures along with lingering college debt.

What I am saying is that avoiding risk is not a less dangerous approach to life than taking risk. Avoiding risk has its own horrific consequences that most people are less aware of because they don't appear in the media reports and are not talked about nearly as much.

Playing it safe is the ultimate attempt at self-preservation. It passes up the opportunity to have an incredibly meaningful life in exchange for mere existence. The sure way to look back in the future with massive regret is to play it safe, be guarded, be suspicious of people who are friendly, assume the worst, and refuse to take chances. Mark Twain said,

"Twenty years from now you will be more disappointed by the things you didn't do than by the ones you did do." That's a big thing for a guy whose life was filled with lots of mischief and adventure to admit.

When you play it safe, you pass up the opportunity to have the conversations that could have changed your life and someone else's. When you play it safe, you never know what was possible. When you play it safe, you lack passion for life, other people don't feel your love, your potential is not discovered, and God's purpose for you goes unfulfilled.

Below are five ways you can be vulnerable and strong at the same time. Together they are examples of how we can risk exposure and open up ourselves mentally, relationally, and spiritually. I put the word *remember* in front of each of them with the hope that you will meditate on them and integrate them into your life.

1. REMEMBER: COMMUNICATION IS NOT JUST A WILLINGNESS TO TALK, BUT AN OPENNESS TO LISTEN.

Leadership by its very nature talks, tells, shares, and gives instruction and direction. Despite all that, without exception I've also found that the best leaders are good listeners. Good listening goes beyond sitting quietly and giving someone your full attention. It also observes and considers what people may not feel comfortable saying. Intuitive leaders put people at ease and lead open, safe, and collaborative conversations. They ask great questions and seek input from the people around them, even those they lead.

I'm often surprised by the vast number of leaders who perceive listening as inferior. Chances are, you won't hear them admit it, but you can tell by their interactions that, at best, they are awkward in a more open and collaborative conversation.

Over the years I've noticed that some people shrink back when I bring them into a peer-level, critical-thinking conversation with others on our team, but then later they ask to tell me their thoughts and opinions privately. It occurred to me that in many of those instances, these individuals wanted to talk but were uncomfortable when being talked back to. One-on-one conversations gave them a chance to tell me what they wanted to say without others being present who might disagree or offer a different opinion. The more I observed this, the more I insisted on having other team members in the room or on the email exchange when processing and making decisions. The more open a team is to reason together and listen to each other, the better their chances are of making great decisions. Instead of talking in corners and not hearing one another, healthy teams are vulnerable and open with each other in their communication.

It's not just leaders who struggle with collaborative, open conversations. Many people retreat, shut down, and are uncomfortable unless they are the one talking. So they play it safe and do all the talking, and eventually they are surrounded by people who have nothing to say. Their spouse, their kids, their friends, the people at work all know they are a one-way conversationalist. They can be commanding as a ruler or withdraw to the window, but they consistently avoid asking the questions, having the conversation, and engaging in collaboration. As commanding as they are, they are never willing to be in the streets.

This is what distinguished David from the rest. Street dancing was part of what made him a strong leader. This is not easy to do when your own former king has thrown spears at you and people you trusted have betrayed you. It's a daily battle, and it takes courage to not retreat to the window. I admire David for this. The fearless way he stayed open and engaged made him a popular leader that mighty men rallied around and common people were eager to follow. Even though many of them never met him or had a conversation with him, they saw that he was strong and vulnerable at the same time, and they loved him for that.

2. REMEMBER: WILLINGNESS TO FAIL WILL ULTIMATELY HELP YOU TO SUCCEED.

Obviously, no one wants to fail at anything, but the more willing you are to fail, the greater chance you have to succeed. If you have a fear of failure, you'll always play it safe and never take the steps necessary to succeed. Once you understand that failing doesn't make you a failure, you will begin to step out more and not take setbacks so personally. You will start to see failing as an essential part of the risk you take on your way to success.

There's a story in the Old Testament about four lepers in Samaria in a time of famine. The only food source was in the neighboring community, where food was being stockpiled by their enemy. These lepers were starving to death. They had every reason to believe that the enemy would not give them food and would kill them if they made any attempt to enter enemy territory. That's when one of the lepers did a risk assessment. He began to question the sanity of staying where they were and dying versus taking the risk of going to the neighboring city in hopes of finding food.

> The more willing you are to fail, the greater chance you have to succeed.

"Why stay here until we die?" he asked (2 Kings 7:3). He wasn't being irrational. He was pointing out the danger of playing it safe. He was saying, *It may be risky to walk toward our enemy, but at least there is the potential for a better life than we'll have if we stay where we are.*

It's true for us as well. The dangerous consequences of playing it safe may be less obvious, but they pose a greater threat in the end. The dangers aren't sudden and dramatic. They develop slowly over time and can be difficult to identify, which is what makes playing it safe more dangerous than the high-profile missteps we hear about or see in the news. Like a slow leak in a tire, the dangers of playing it safe aren't something we see or feel on a daily basis. We become aware of them only when we realize we're stuck and wondering how it happened. That's when we take note of the bigger picture and realize that playing it safe isn't as safe as it appears to be.

What I love about the story of the four lepers is that heaven suddenly backed them up when they finally made their gutsy move to stand to their feet and begin walking in the direction of food. When they headed into enemy territory, God caused the enemy to hear loud, thunderlike noises, which they thought were the chariots and horses of an army coming to attack them. The enemy fled for their lives, leaving behind everything, including the food that they had stockpiled. The four lepers walked into the city and found it vacated and filled with plenty of food, not only for themselves but also for the people of Israel.

This is what happens when we have the courage to not stay where we are or as we are even if it means risking failure. Acts of faith always attract God's attention and cause Him to move mightily on our behalf. This doesn't happen when we sit in safe places. It only happens when we dare to move in the direction of our dreams.

3. REMEMBER: YOU CAN'T MAKE A GREAT DECISION UNLESS YOU MAKE A DECISION.

Indecision is one of the most common ways people play it safe. Rather than being like the four lepers who put themselves out there, risking the results of a bad decision, most people convince themselves that indecision is a safe decision. They tell themselves that not making a commitment to a specific direction in their life is better because it leaves their options open. The truth is that there is risk either way.

There are times in our lives when we have to make decisions even when we're not sure which direction to go. Scripture says, "By faith Abraham, when called to go to a place he would later receive as his inheritance, obeyed and went, even though he did not know where he was going" (Heb. 11:8).

We gather as many facts as we can, consider the options, ask God for wisdom, and then use our best judgment and the insight of others to guide us forward. Once we make our decision, we have to be willing to stick with it and not allow fear and second-guessing to derail us. We have to stop focusing on the what-ifs and instead concentrate all of our energy on taking the steps needed to be successful.

Start moving in the direction of your decision and focus your attention that way. You won't have your best experience looking in the rearview mirror. Just like driving an automobile, you can benefit by an occasional glance back, but looking forward and staying focused on where you're going is the only way you can expect to get there.

The reality is that you only have to make a few great decisions in order to have an exceptional life—and you can't make a great decision unless you make an actual decision. For our twenty-fifth wedding anniversary Sheila and I decided to tour around Switzerland and Italy for about ten days. Once we knew where we were going, we could decide how we were going to get there, who we were going with, how we were going to get around while we were there, and where we were going to stay. Some of the decisions we made in preparation changed once we were there in the moment, but we wouldn't have been able to pivot to a new and better decision if we hadn't made the decision to be there in the first place. The same is true in your life. Once you decide where you are going as a person—as a parent, as a husband or wife, in your career, in your relationship with God—there are other decisions to make, but they become a lot less complicated once you know where you're going.

Get comfortable with the fact that every decision you make will not be a great decision, but at least you're on the road to making actual, real decisions.

4. REMEMBER: GETTING HURT IS UNAVOIDABLE, BUT STAYING HURT IS OPTIONAL.

The biggest reason people play it safe? They assume they can avoid getting hurt…again. They refer to a past marriage, the "other" church, or the last friend they trusted who let them down, and they vow to not let it happen again. What they don't realize is that while they think they are *avoiding* hurt, they are actually *still* hurt and *staying* hurt. Staying hurt means *living* hurt. If you're living hurt, you aren't trying to avoid getting hurt—you are hurt! That's like someone with both arms in casts saying, *I'm not going to let someone break my arm.*

The truth is that it's impossible to avoid getting hurt. In

fact, the only way to avoid pain is to avoid living. We're much better off embracing pain as a part of life than spending our energy trying to avoid it. Pain never leaves us like we were. It always changes us. The good news is that we determine how it changes us. When we get hurt, we can call it the story of our life, or we can move forward and say it was just a chapter in our life. We can choose to say, "I'm not turning inward; I'm turning upward. I'm not going to let the rejection, the criticism, the embarrassment, make me bitter. It's going to make me better!"

When we decide to live like this, we begin to realize that forgiveness is our friend. It's not about doing someone else a favor by forgiving them—it's about doing ourselves a favor by forgiving those who've hurt us. Life is at its best when we're recovering quickly, overlooking the small stuff, believing the best, and staying healthy emotionally, spiritually, and physically. We don't have to let the hurt of our past mess up the hope of our future!

5. REMEMBER: YOU CAN'T PLAY IT SAFE AND ACT IN FAITH AT THE SAME TIME.

At a meeting of church leaders in the late 1700s, a newly ordained minister stood to argue for the value of overseas missions. He was abruptly interrupted by an older minister who said, "Young man, sit down! You are an enthusiast. When God pleases to convert the heathen, he'll do it without consulting you or me."

The reason that attitude is inconceivable today is largely due to the subsequent efforts of that young man, William Carey. Carey worked in various jobs to support his family while he continued to educate himself, even teaching himself New Testament Greek. In 1792 he organized a missionary society, and at the first gathering he preached a sermon with the call "Expect great things from God; attempt great things for God!" Within a year, Carey, his family, and some like-minded daring people were on a ship headed for India.

In many ways, Carey was the catalyst for change, helping to inspire a big-thinking, risk-taking, faith-filled approach to modern missions. He served the rest of his life in India at a time where there was no modern travel or communication systems. He was a minister, translator, social reformer and cultural anthropologist who founded the Serampore College and the Serampore University, the first degree-awarding university in India. Carey even translated the Bible into Bengali, Oriya, Marathi, Hindi, Assamese, and Sanskrit. He also translated parts of it into twenty-nine other languages and dialects. He helped educate horticulturists, which raised the quality and productivity of the nation's agricultural industry. His life was a living, breathing example that big things happen when we expect great things from God and attempt great things for God.[1]

Our tendency is to make decisions that we are comfortable with, to play it safe and do only what we feel is rational.

But God has called us to acts of faith. We're not meant to spend our lives as mere observers and spectators who hang out in the bleachers and offer commentary as world events play out in front of us. We're here to engage potential, explore possibilities, and *act* in faith.

Scripture tells us, "we do not belong to those who shrink back and are destroyed, but to those who have faith and are saved" (Heb. 10:39). If you're a Jesus follower, this applies to everything God has for you. When you have challenges, setbacks, even failures and mess-ups, you are not meant to be like those who shrink back. No, you are meant to take on the challenge and push through resistance that tries to contain you.

When you don't pass the entrance exam or get accepted into the college you applied for, don't shrink back. When you feel small or unqualified, don't shrink back. When you don't get noticed by your spouse, when the promotion you hoped for doesn't come through, or when you feel discouraged by how your kids are acting, don't shrink back. God has something for you and needs you to keep walking by faith. Remind yourself that big things happen when you act in faith. Keep going big. Keep believing in what you don't see. Pray bold prayers. Your life story will be dramatically different with acts of faith. Doors will open that would otherwise stay closed. Relationships with like-minded people and God-assigned connections will happen that would have otherwise never happened. When you live out of faith and not in fear, you will accomplish more, experience greater fulfillment, and leave a lasting legacy.

Chances are you're not called to be a missionary like William Carey. Nor are you meant to walk the path of Condoleezza Rice, or for that matter anyone else in history. If you're like most of us who have a tendency to play it safe, God may use this book to make your safe place feel dangerous. You just might find yourself starting to choose acts of faith in your everyday life. Rather than just seeing a need, you may start to see the opportunity. Rather than just thinking, *Why doesn't someone do something?*, you may find yourself saying, *I'm going to do something.*

Expect great things from God and attempt great things for God. You won't regret it!

Study Questions

1. Why is playing it safe dangerous?
2. Think of someone you know who lives boldly. What do you admire about people who take risks?
3. Discuss or reflect on this quote from chapter 3: "Playing it safe is the ultimate attempt at self-preservation. It passes up the opportunity to have an incredibly meaningful life in exchange for mere existence."
4. Think of a time you regret that you played it safe and avoided risk. What would you do differently next time?
5. Consider an example when someone acted in faith and how it attracted heaven to get involved in that situation.

CHAPTER 4

COMFORT IS WAY OVERRATED

In *The Lego Movie 2: The Second Part*, the main character, Emmet, is challenged to get tougher and see the world through a darker perspective. However, he comes to the conclusion that hardening his heart and isolating himself is actually the easy thing to do, while being vulnerable and positive is tough but worth it. He says, "It's easy to harden your heart, but to open it is the toughest thing we can do."[1]

As author Brené Brown says, "We can choose courage or we can choose comfort, but we can't have both." At least, not at the same time, which is why comfort is way overrated. We don't get stronger by staying comfortable. We get stronger physically when we head to the gym and pick up the weights or go for a run until our muscles are tired, our lungs have been stretched, and our body is begging us to please stop. It's the same way when it comes to broadening our relationships or developing our competence. The only way we get stronger is by putting ourselves in the places that push us out of our comfort zone socially, mentally, or spiritually. The best things in life don't come from being comfortable.

Ask a pregnant woman if she's comfortable, and you might get slapped! No, she's not comfortable, but that's not to be expected when having a baby. Just like babies are formed in pressure, diamonds are firmed in pressure. Pushing past our comfort zones puts us in a place of pressure. We're face-to-face with the possibilities of embarrassment, failure, disappointment, or inadequacy. This pressure is part of the process. Why do it? Because pressure is where diamonds are formed and babies are born.

Being vulnerable is being brave enough to put yourself in uncomfortable places, places where there are no guarantees that it's going to work out like you hope it does. It's having the courage to put yourself out there when there is a risk and you have no control over the outcome. When you're in high school, putting yourself out there might be asking someone to go with you to the prom. *What if she says no? I'm going to look stupid in front of my friends.* The hesitation is based on the fact that you're making yourself vulnerable to rejection, and that's scary to you. When we get past the dating thing, vulnerability looks different, but it always requires courage. It can be starting your own business, volunteering to lead a team at church, or moving to a different city without having a job lined up. While we want comfort, we crave the things that only courage can give.

When David removed his robe, he was doing what other kings would feel uncomfortable doing. He was setting aside his status so that he could be free in his worship. He wanted to celebrate. He wanted to dance in the streets. This is who David was. He was a street dancer. But on this day it required a lot of courage for David to get beyond who others expected him to be so he could be who he was meant to be.

> While we want comfort, we crave the things that only courage can give.

Wanting comfort explains why we all wear "robes," metaphorically speaking. Robes that hide what we don't want others to know about us and help us present a version of ourselves to the people around us that we want them to see. There are things about us that we don't like, so we assume that if others really knew us they wouldn't like us. We convince ourselves that they would think badly of us and reject us. That's where the robe comes in, and it also explains why removing the robe can cause us to feel afraid.

When you spend your whole life presenting the version of yourself that you want others to see, it's a scary venture to start removing your robes. To call all robe wearing hypocrisy is not fair or accurate. There was nothing wrong with King David wearing the robe of royalty. There was also nothing wrong with him putting his armor on to go into battle.

Robe wearing is a sensible and even necessary part of our interaction with others. The problem starts when the robe rules you instead of serving you. That's when the robe has to be removed, because it can get in the way of you being who God created you to be. There's only one you. God can't bless who you pretend to be. He can only bless who you are designed to be.

Even though David was the first king in his family—regardless of people's expectations—he wasn't willing to part ways with his authentic self. The music-making, worship-singing, street-dancing David changed his address from shepherd fields to the royal palace, but he remained steadfast in his love for God and the common people of Jerusalem. In the same way that David's assignment was unique to him, your assignment is unique to you. The only option for those of us who want to live out our assignment and be all we are meant to be is to do what David did: wear the robe loose and always be ready to remove it when it gets in the way. Stay intentional about never confusing who you are with the robe you wear.

When we come into the world we come in naked and unafraid. Babies don't need clothes on to make them feel secure. They walk around in their earth suit without any need to cover up. No apology, no insecurity, no fear of what someone might think. But usually by the time we start school we have learned to be embarrassed without our clothes on. We have officially become self-conscious. We start to wonder what other people think about us. That's where the robe wearing begins. It begins as an effort to either conform to or reject the social norms and expectations of those around us, which is why everyone wears robes. The robes serve us well and help us maintain dignity in social settings and re-lational environments. But the robes can also separate us from our unique and authentic self.

One reason so many people struggle to know who they are meant to be is that they have spent all their life being who they are *supposed* to be. All their life they've tried to measure up to the expectations of those around them. Most of us have a whole closet full of robes that we have worn at one time or another in an attempt to fit in, follow protocol, and meet expectations.

When our robes start to dictate the choices we make, the freedom we have, the joy we feel, and the expressions we give, that's when the robes have to come off.

When a robe gets in the way of us connecting and doing life in community, it has to come off.

When a robe causes us to confuse who others say we have to be with who we are meant to be, it has to come off.

When a robe hinders us from putting our whole heart into serving God, it has to come off.

When a robe causes us to withdraw into observation ver-sus a life of participation, it has to come off.

When a robe causes us to close up or shut down emotion-ally, it has to come off.

When a robe keeps us from having fun and enjoying life, it has to come off.

When a robe makes us self-conscious and afraid of what people are saying and thinking about us, it has to come off.

When a robe stops us from expressing our love for God, family, and friends, it has to come off.

When a robe becomes our cover-up for past pain that God wants to heal, it has to come off.

When a robe makes us shrink back from opportunities, it has to come off.

When a robe makes us unapproachable, it has to come off.

When a robe turns us into a poser or pretender, it has to come off.

When a robe causes pride and disconnects us from the people God connected us with, it has to come off.

Michal criticized David for removing his royal robe, and she felt safe in the window. But remember, staying in the window is *not* safe; it only *feels* safe. If you stay in the window, relationships remain shallow, intimacy is impossible, freedom from fear is never experienced, God's purpose is not fulfilled, your potential is never discovered, and your best life is never lived.

STREET LIFE

For David, removing the robe seemed to be the only natural and appropriate response in that moment. He recognized that the Ark of the Covenant being returned to Jerusalem represented the opportunity of a lifetime. A dream that was in process. A doorway into the future. David was determined to not miss the moment. You have to know that life is best when comfort is not the goal, hesitation is not your habit, and complacency is your enemy. Life in the streets is about cause, not applause. It's about responding to the opportunity, joining the team, being all in on the mission. It's about leaving the cheap seats, getting out of the bleachers, and heading for the field. It's raising your hand to volunteer at church, serve in community, and live to make a difference. This is what Theodore Roosevelt did when he stepped out to take on the cynics of his time who were looking down on those who were trying to make the world a better place.

On April 23, 1910, Theodore Roosevelt gave a speech titled "The Man in the Arena." It would become one of the most widely quoted speeches of his career. "The poorest way to face life is to face it with a sneer," he said. "A cynical habit of thought and speech, a readiness to criticize work which the critic himself never tries to perform, an intellectual aloofness which will not accept contact with life's realities—all these are marks, not...of superiority but of weakness." His message was inspirational and passionate:

> It is not the critic who counts; not the man who points out how the strong man stumbles, or where the doer of deeds could have done them better. The credit belongs to the man who is actually in the arena, whose face is marred by dust and sweat and blood; who strives valiantly; who errs, who comes up short again and again, because there is no effort without error and shortcoming; but who does actually strive to do the deeds; who knows great enthusiasms, the great devotions; who spends himself in a worthy cause; who at the best knows in the end the triumph of high achievement, and who at

the worst, if he fails, at least fails while daring greatly, so that his place shall never be with those cold and timid souls who neither know victory nor defeat.[2]

In much the same way, our lives are filled with God-given opportunities that deserve to be met with an uninhibited display of openness and readiness. In order to live fully free, here's what you have to know with absolute certainty and complete confidence: *The best life is the street life.*

Study Questions

1. Discuss or reflect on this quote: "We can choose courage or we can choose comfort, but we can't have both." How does this affect your everyday life?
2. In what area of your life do you need to leave the comfort zone?
3. Look back in this chapter at the list of robes that people use to cover up (page 41). What robe are you wearing that needs to come off?
4. Since life in the streets is about cause and not applause, what is a cause that gets you fired up and passionate?

ABANDON SMALLNESS

"We didn't fence you in. The smallness you feel comes from within you."

—Apostle Paul

"Life is too short to be little."

—Benjamin Disraeli

CHAPTER 5

GROWING BIGGER ON THE INSIDE

We're not sure what went through David's mind when a servant came running to the fields where he was watching his father's sheep and said, "The prophet Samuel wants to see you." It's safe to assume, however, that as the youngest son placed last on the "most likely to be chosen" list, his heart started pounding as he headed toward the front lawn of his father's house, where the prophet, his father, and his brothers were all waiting for him (1 Sam. 16). He was probably still short of breath from the fast-paced journey when Samuel motioned for him to come stand in front of him. This was his first job interview, except he hadn't even applied for the job. There he was on a stage with the highly revered prophet and his whole family looking on. His brothers now knew that the sequence in the line seemed to be shifting. Maybe some of them felt relieved, but it's likely that some of them felt a sudden rush of disbelief and amazement that David could be suddenly in line ahead of them. No doubt David's palms were sweaty and his head was saying, *This can't be happening! I'm young, I lack experience— surely there are others more qualified than I am.*

At the same time, there was another conversation going on in that same moment as God talked to Samuel about Eliab, the older, physically stronger, bigger brother of David: "Do not look on his appearance or on the height of his stature, because I have rejected him." Then the Lord said in reference to David, "The LORD does not see as mortals see; they look on the outward appearance, but the LORD looks on the heart" (1 Sam. 16:7 NRSV). Then, as if it had been rehearsed ahead of time, the horn of anointing oil was uncapped and Samuel prophetically poured it over David's head as a way of declaring him first in line to become the next king of Israel.

It's helpful to understand that as sacred as that moment was, it meant that David was chosen only, but not yet announced. He was privately positioned, but now began the process of preparation. This was God's plan all along. David would not be recognized by others at this point as being more than a shepherd, a son of Jesse. Being chosen as king did not mean he didn't have to continue the process of being proven. The same is true for you.

Having an assignment on your life doesn't mean you can bypass the preparation process. God has designed your life to have proving grounds of opportunity, places and spaces where you are given the chance to arrive at one level as a doorway to something greater. This is why it's important to not back away when opportunity knocks, when you suddenly find yourself in unfamiliar territory that you feel unprepared for. When this happens it's likely that you are in a proving ground intended to stretch you beyond where you are and prepare you for something bigger ahead. As uncomfortable as you might feel being stretched, the consequence of staying as you are is that you miss out on the bigger life God has for you.

GROWING ON THE INSIDE

God had big plans for David, but David had some growing to do, not just physically, but internally. The only way David could go where God wanted him to go was for him to grow to the point where God could trust him with responsibility to lead not only sheep but his people. Physical growth is something everyone can see in real time, but internal growth happens in quiet places and becomes visible when opportunity comes and demand is placed on it. In the case of David, the opportunity given him was the job of caring for and protecting his father's sheep. No one knew what David was ready for until predators threatened his father's sheep. It was then that his courage and confidence became visible. His courage and poise showed up in adversity.

Adversity doesn't just make you strong, it reveals the strength—or lack of—that's already there. God has a bigger life for you! He has plans to use your past and current circumstances not only for your good but for the benefit of others. Every challenge, every battle, every test, and every victory becomes an experience that God can use to enlarge your capacity for more.

If you're in a shepherd field now, that doesn't mean you are meant to be there forever. If you are in obscurity now, that doesn't mean you always will be. Where you are now is part of the *process of preparation* for where God is taking you later. In and of itself, what you are experiencing now may seem to lack purpose, like a piece of a puzzle that on its own is confusing until it gets connected into the bigger picture. The season that you don't understand is an opportunity to trust God that the pieces, even the odd ones, are going to come together to fulfill his purpose in you.

Scripture says, "*If* you faint in the day of adversity, your strength *is* small" (Prov. 24:10 NKJV; emphasis added). It doesn't say we faint because of the size of the adversity. It says we faint because of the smallness of our strength. We can't do anything about the size of the adversity, but we can do something about the size of our strength. We can think bigger, pray bigger, have greater courage, have a bigger vision, increase our knowledge, and grow our faith. Living small doesn't help you or anyone else, and it doesn't bring glory to God. You can hold on to smallness or abandon it. The choice is yours. Best-selling author Marianne Williamson says it like this: "Our deepest fear is that we are powerful beyond measure. It is our light, not our darkness, that most frightens us…Your playing small does not serve the world. There is nothing enlightened about shrinking so that other people won't feel insecure around you."[1]

> We can't do anything about the size of the adversity, but we can do something about the size of our strength.

This is something most of us need to be reminded of on a regular basis. To not shrink the greatness and potential in our own life to accommodate someone else's insecurity. Your going small won't cause someone who is insecure to be more confident. It will only cause you to shrink the greatness inside of you. I'm not suggesting you be insensitive to those who are insecure. But I am hoping to convince you that there are consequences in shrinking yourself to accommodate the insecurities of those around you. First of all, when you shrink to the size of those who are insecure it doesn't make them more secure. Secondly, when you reduce your confidence, you'll compromise your calling. You can't do what God's given you to do if you cast away your confidence. Scripture challenges us, "So do not throw away your confidence; it will be richly rewarded" (Heb. 10:35). The writer is saying life is different with confidence than without it. Confidence doesn't just make us feel better, it makes our life better!

Most of David's life was shepherding his father's sheep, which meant being alone while staying alert. It was back-to-back days of mundane, boring sheep counting. Any time you are doing something alone, you can go one of two ways. You can underestimate the significance of what you're doing and become apathetic toward your boring, mundane life, or you can go big in a seemingly small, insignificant season of your life, push outside your comfort zone, and go beyond your current experience and skills to create an impressive résumé for your future.

That's what David did. He turned an otherwise boring task into a self-development classroom. He learned to be open and expressive toward God. He learned to try new things like writing songs and playing music. He took pride in the role he had been given and spent hours slinging stones at pretend predators, knowing real predators would be coming after the sheep. He was there, faithful in his role to protect them. He had grown in bravery and in his skills. In the hills of obscurity, David had gone face-to-face with lions and bears that came looking for a rack of lamb. God had seen that David had the potential to push past his own comfort zone for the benefit of the greater victory. Up until now, when given the opportunity "to go big or go home," he wasn't one who was seeking comfort or playing it safe. Whether it was a bear coming after his father's sheep or fear coming after his heart, David repeatedly met the moment with the poise of a seasoned, skilled fighter.

If you want to create something that matters, for both yourself and others, you have to start where you are, with what you have. That's how you build momentum over time. You push past your own comfort zone for the benefit of the greater glory. Where others see the mundane and minimize it, you see the possibility and maximize it. It's the difference between artists and entrepreneurs who get lucky once and those who sustain success over decades.

If you cling to what got you there in the first place, you'll fail to evolve, and you will render yourself irrelevant. We could all probably think of some one-hit wonders of the world—they sang a song that went viral, granting them instant fame, and then they never sang another song to rival their first. Success is only sustainable by putting yourself out there again and again. Whether it's in relationships or in your life's work, the only way to keep getting stronger is to keep being vulnerable.

For David, the shepherd field was a place of great beginnings, but what was big to him in the shepherd field was small compared to God's plans for his future. It's the same way for us. The bigger life is never forced upon us; it's only offered to us. The key is not to allow self-imposed limits where God has given wide-open spaces. Push those limits aside and see what God will do with your life!

MINI-ME

My dad and I shared a secret between us that he said Mom wasn't supposed to know about because she wouldn't understand. The first time I remember talking about it was when we lived on Lambeth Lane in a small rambler house within a circle at the end of the street. The cul-de-sac was an advantage for us kids because it meant we could use the street as our playground. The only traffic we got was from the people who lived there, the mailman, and the snow cone truck that came through every day in the summer.

I couldn't have been more than seven or eight when Dad drove into the driveway one day just in time to see me coming down the street headed toward our house. He could tell something was wrong. As I crossed the lawn headed toward the front door, he began calling for me and asking what was wrong. About that time I started to cry, but it wasn't my dad I wanted to see. I wanted my mom. As I ran into the house looking for her, my dad came in right behind me. The next few minutes I was a sobbing mess as I told my parents how the boy down the street had hit me and called me names again. This wasn't the first time it had happened, and neither was it the first time I'd sought refuge in my mother's arms.

It was that day, after mom had done what moms do, that Dad did what good dads do. After Mom left the room, there in that small living room, Dad started to talk to the "mini-me," the "weaker" version of myself. He told me I didn't have to let the other kid bully me. He reminded me that he and I wrestled and boxed, and that I didn't have to let any of the other boys push me around. He gave me permission to stand up, be bigger, and fight back. He told me to never start a fight, but to never run away from one. If he ever found out that I started a fight, he would "whup" me when I got home. But if another boy pushed me or started a fight with me, I should give him a "whuppin'," or my dad would give me one when I got home. My dad came from a family tree of rough Cajun characters in southern Louisiana, and I knew exactly what he meant when he said "whuppin'." Mom would never have told me to do any of that, so Dad made sure I knew that this conversation was between us.

Looking back, I know that my dad was not just giving me permission to fight; he was giving me permission to become the bigger me. He was calling out the stronger me, the tougher me, the fighter in me. Before then, the mini-me didn't even know there was a bigger me. I didn't know that I could stand up for myself, face fear, and fight back. The mini-me had lived in a small, protected, safe world, coddled in comfort.

Although my dad gave me permission to stand up for myself, I still had to work past the fear of what would happen when I did. That was the last time I ran home to my mom, but it's not the last time I had to deal with my own mini-me.

What makes smallness difficult to overcome is that it feels easier and more comfortable than pressing forward into your dreams. Comfort zones are the places where dreams go to die. There have been countless times when my feelings of smallness were in direct opposition to the God-given opportunities in front of me. And I had to embrace the call, as you will need to do, to be the fighter God was calling me to be.

SMALLNESS VERSUS BIGNESS

Shortly after I came to the Pacific Northwest to pastor a small church, I went with a friend to hear popular evangelist Reinhard Bonnke speak. When we got there, the only seats were in the very top of the stadium seating. The domed building seemed so massive, and yet the bigness in me whispered, *Wouldn't it be great to have a big building like this full of worshipping people?* For whatever reason, that night it seemed completely possible that someday I would have a building like that.

> Comfort zones are the places where dreams go to die.

The amazing thing is that a few years later, I didn't just have a building *like* that building; I had that *exact building*! Everything we imagine isn't supposed to happen, but God uses our imagination to stretch us, prepare us, and encourage us toward the bigger life He has planned for us. This is why you don't want to get stuck in pettiness or trivial arguments. Your life is too important and has too much potential to get sidetracked in strife or offense. Instead, stay focused on the bigger picture of possibility that is in front of you. Being big is what keeps the doors of opportunity open for God to work in your life!

Scripture says that God "is able to do exceeding abundantly above all that we ask or think, according to the power that works in us" (Eph. 3:20 NKJV). The bigness inside of us is the power that works in us to keep us open and in sync with God's plans for us. As you keep reading, tell yourself, *I'm made in the image of God. There's bigness inside of me. There's untapped power inside of me.* If you start believing that, you will sense the "bigger you" coming alive within you. *Smallness betrays us, and bigness befriends us.*

> Being big is what keeps the doors of opportunity open for God to work in your life!

When I listen to my mini-me, it coaches me into small-ness. It tells me to keep my guard up and play it safe. It points toward past examples where I've been disappointed by people. It reminds me of my own failures—times when I overreached or tried too hard to make something happen. The voice of my mini-me is often very reasonable, which is what makes it so persuasive. But it can also be petty and un-forgiving and focus exclusively on the negative.

Without fail, when I listen to that mini-me, I always have regrets. Sometimes it's only a day later, and other times it's weeks, months, or even years down the road. But without exception, every time I go small, I look back with regret, knowing that that voice betrayed me. It shut me down, took away my power, and left me wondering what could have happened if I had not listened to it.

On the other hand, when I listen to the bigger me, it coaches me in the opposite direction. It tells me to live fear-lessly. To not allow past disappointments to abort today's possibilities. To see that everything is working together for my good. The bigger me refuses to be petty and insists that I look for the good in everything. It points me toward the people who love me, stick with me, encourage me, and are there for me. It reminds me that those relationships are priceless and are products of my own willingness to press into people, believe in them, love, take risks, and be open to the possibility of friendship and relationship.

When I go big, without exception I always look back with gratitude that I listened to the bigger me. Regardless of how things turn out, I always feel a sense of fulfillment knowing that I gave it my best and didn't back down. That positive belief helps me to keep living from the bigness God has put within me—the confidence that He provides through His promises and presence in my life.

I'm not the only one who comes in two sizes—small and large. All of us have the ability to go small or big. Which voice we follow determines how far we will go.

WHAT FITS NOW WILL HURT LATER

We were in a sports shoe store and my then-eight-year-old grandson, Kyan, was loving the new blue Steph Curry shoes. The first pair he tried on were too small; his toes were pushing into the toe of the shoe. He asked the salesperson if there was a bigger size. When she returned, she apologized that they didn't have the next half size, and so she brought out a full size bigger. He put them on, but since they were a bit too big, he reverted back to the smaller size. He was right when he said that the smaller size felt better. But what he wasn't considering when wanting to go with the smaller size was what we all deal with when it's time to get bigger on the inside: Small feels good in the moment, but it hurts us in the future.

You might remember as a kid when your parents made you tell someone you were sorry for something you did. Remember how hard that was? That's a snapshot of what it's like when we're pushing ourselves to get bigger on the inside. In the moment, bigger feels awkward and uncomfortable, but later on it serves you well. As Kyan walked around the store, he was like an attorney making his case that the smaller ones didn't hurt his feet and were a good fit for him. He didn't want to go bigger. Over the next few minutes, we managed to convince him that if he wanted the shoes, the bigger ones were the best choice. He walked out in the bigger ones, which provided plenty of room for him to grow.

For the sake of clarity, let me show you how internal smallness affects us in a number of ways:

- It causes us to be self-conscious.
- It causes us to be slow to compliment and encourage others.
- It causes us to be slow to celebrate the wins of other people.
- It causes us to engage in petty and negative conversations where people complain, gossip, and criticize.
- It causes us to be envious of other people's success.
- It causes us to shrink ourselves to stay as small a target as possible so the world won't shoot us down.
- It causes us to pass up opportunities to contribute—being careful not to put ourselves out there where we risk saying the wrong thing or having our ideas rejected by the group.

- It causes us to take things too personally.
- It causes us to assume the worst in people or about people.
- It causes us to put the focus on what we want to avoid—pain, confrontation, and embarrassment—instead of what we want to accomplish.
- It causes us to let criticism lay us low rather than help us grow.
- It causes us to be inhibited to love out loud—not free to say love, show love, or feel love.
- It causes us to turn inward, shut down, and withdraw emotionally.
- It causes us to make excuses rather than owning our choices, our moods, and our behavior.

I'm sure when you look at this list, at least some of these are habits that feel harmless right now in your own life. If so, this is your window logic. You're so intent on being comfortable in the moment that you're willing to overlook the consequences in the future. All window logic is like a pair of snug tennis shoes on an eight-year-old. It fits now and hurts later.

When you look around you for people who model bigness, it's not always easy to differentiate between those who appear to be big on the inside and those who actually are. Being big on the inside is not the same as being popular, being wealthy, or having a big personality. In fact, some of the most popular, wealthy, and big-personality people are small inside. Once you get past the outer layer of their positions and persona, you often see their internal struggle with smallness. You start to see glimpses of their struggle with insecurity. You start to hear about who bothers them, what worries them, what they dread most, what irritates them, and what triggers a bad mood or even a paranoia of some kind. They can be petty, have issues with other people, carry grudges from the past, and have a hard time celebrating the success of others.

On the other hand, there are people who are just the opposite. When you first look at them, you see them as pretty average. They don't have big personalities; they are not loud or the center of attention. The more you get to know them, the more you start to see glimpses of unusual confidence and courage. You start to realize how positive they are in their conversations. They think well and speak well of others. They believe the best about the future. They don't take themselves too seriously. They are uncomplicated, have a genuine love for life, and are comfortable putting themselves out there as if they have nothing to lose.

THE BIGGER YOU

Maybe you're unaware of the bigger you waiting to be given permission to speak up, to help out, to take you to new places of faith and confidence that the smallness inside you has held you back from. Maybe you're unaware of your untapped possibilities, untrained talent, and undeveloped strengths. If so, you're not alone.

I was in a conversation recently with a twenty-eight-year-old man who shared how his father had abandoned him and his mother when he was a young boy. He told me how he had reached out to his dad at various times but was repeatedly disappointed when his dad always found reasons to avoid spending time with him. He described how he looks back now and realizes how his father's rejection caused him to fall into a pattern of rejecting other people along the way when they reached out to him or showed interest in him. He said he wished he could go back and respond differently to those people, because he now realizes that he missed out on opportunities for relationships with people that God had sent into his life to help him. In the moment that he didn't return the call or respond to the text message, he wasn't sure why he wasn't responding, but now he recognizes that his fear of being rejected by others like he had been rejected by his father was holding him back and causing him to miss out on what God had for him. That's how the mini-me minimizes the value of a God-assigned connection. While we're wrapped up in a self-protective and guarded position, there are people God is sending into our lives. The way we treat the people God sends our way determines whether or not they will stay.

What I enjoyed most about this man's story was how he made the decision to push past his pain, identify his fears, and then give himself permission to get bigger on the inside. He now has a son of his own, and he is excited to give his son all the love he missed out on. He also has a career working with troubled youth. This is what it looks like to move from a mini-me to a bigger me.

Refuse to settle in conditions that you are designed to transcend and rise above. There's a bigger you that just needs permission to rise above the trap of small-minded conversations that you have been having with yourself. The decision to abandon smallness begins when you give yourself permission on a constant, daily basis to grow bigger on the inside. You can start today to change the internal dialogue and those petty conversations to big-thinking, risk-taking, faith-filled devotion to God's big plans for your life.

Study Questions

1. What are some ways people can challenge themselves to grow bigger on the inside?
2. Look at the list describing internal smallness on page 59. Which ones resonate with you the most?
3. Have you ever held back from your full potential to accommodate someone else? If so, why?
4. Are you currently in a process of preparation? What are some identifiers you are aware of now?

CHAPTER 6

GETTING BEYOND THE FEAR FENCE

The African impala is well known for its remarkable leap-ing ability—it can jump ten feet high and thirty feet long. You would assume that zookeepers would have a tough time keeping impalas in their enclosures, but much shorter walls—sometimes only three feet tall—work to keep them in. Why? Because impalas will not jump if they cannot see where they will land.

Impalas flee in the wild when a lion appears. The fear that makes them run from a predator is not the same fear that holds them behind zoo walls. One fear is a fear of being eaten. The other fear—a fear that holds them back from what they're capable of doing—is due to the fact that they can't see their next step clearly.

All smallness is dictated by some type of fear. These fears act like a fence that holds us in a limited mindset that makes us feel safe. These are not the same kinds of fear we feel when our life is suddenly in danger. It's different from the panic of being on a plane when the engine goes out or you hear someone breaking into your house in the middle of the night. It's not the same as being in the mountains of Alaska and coming face-to-face with a bear who sees you as God's provision at mealtime.

No. The kind of fear that holds people in a place of smallness is a different form of fear. It's more subtle and harder to recognize. We might call it a hesitation, a concern, an apprehension, or an inhibition. It might cause us to opt out of things by saying it's something we don't like or just don't want to do. As we tune in and are more honest about our fears, we may start to put names to the specific fears that fence us in: the fear of inadequacy, the fear of rejection, and the fear of failure. These are the kinds of fears that make us timid, which is what the apostle Paul saw and referred to in his protégé Timothy, "For God has not given us a spirit of fear and timidity, but of power, love, and self-discipline" (2 Tim. 1:7 NLT). If we want to live a life of purpose, we have to know that God has not given us a spirit of fear and timidity.

Remember, being vulnerable means making a move when there is no guarantee of the outcome. Leaping when you can't see where you will land. Rather than imagining the worst, imagine the best. Rather than worrying about what people will think or say about us or what happens if we fail, we can focus on attempting great things for God and expecting great things from God. There's no doubt that street dancing can be scary for anyone. But it's even more scary to think that maybe you've unknowingly embraced fear as a mentor in your life.

It may sound overstated at first, but the truth is that the greatest things you can do in life are scary.

- When you graduate high school and start considering college, it can be scary.
- When you head out to find a job or do an interview, it can be scary.
- When you sign up to serve your country, it can be scary.
- When you are getting ready to get married, it can be scary.
- When you start a business, it can be scary.
- When you plant a church, it can be scary.

Remember, fear happens to everyone when they start to push past the comfortable and the familiar. It happens when you risk exposure. When you decide to do something new, something you've never done before, you can't avoid feeling fear. The fence you built to protect yourself from the outside world is now the fence that holds you hostage. It tells you to stay in its boundaries and you'll be safe. It tells you that if you venture outside its boundaries, there's no guarantee of a positive outcome. So, the questions you have to consider are these: *Does the pressing need to protect yourself really benefit you? Does it get you what you long for in life? Does it make you feel strong? Or is it just the opposite? Do you feel strong when you're taking the chance, pressing in, and risking exposure?*

The question is not, *Do we feel a need to protect ourselves?*

There's no question about that—of course we do. The question is, *Do we want to let that urge of self-preservation, that inevitable feeling of fear, fence us in and hold us back?*

One study, based on brain-imaging technology, enabled neuroscientists to prove that we are wired to overestimate the size of risk and underestimate our ability to handle it.[1] The result is that we are often driven by our fear of what we don't want rather than a commitment to what we do want.

We don't want to be embarrassed.

We don't want to be rejected.

We don't want to be a failure.

We don't want to lose what we have.

We don't want to be alone.

We don't want to be misunderstood.

When fear fences us in, we exhaust our thoughts and energy protecting ourselves rather than advancing ourselves. None of us feel as good when we're in self-protective mode as we do when we are focused on taking the next steps to move in the direction of our dreams. Yes, ships are safe in the harbor, but they are meant for open waters. A plane may be safer on the tarmac, but it's meant to fly.

From the Old Testament straight through to the teachings of Jesus and the apostles, Scripture urges us to abandon smallness and live free and expansive, big-thinking, faith-filled lives. We are encouraged to leave behind the trappings of worry, doubt, and fear. Those things don't fit us as believers. They don't look or feel good on us. As Christ followers, we're called to believe in things we don't see and to speak of things that are not yet. We're called to acts of faith. You and I are designed to walk by faith and not by sight.

In fact, there may be no call more consistent in Scripture than the call to abandon the trappings of smallness that hold us back from the great things God has for us. This small mindset is what the apostle Paul was addressing when he wrote to believers in the sixth chapter of 2 Corinthians. He starts by saying, God has given us a "marvelous life" (2 Cor. 6:1 MSG)—not a small or insignificant life—a *marvelous* life that deserves to be lived ambitiously and fully. Then he talks specifically about the fence that fear builds: "Dear, dear Corinthians, I can't tell you how much I long for you to enter this wide-open, spacious life. We didn't fence you in. The smallness you feel comes from within you. Your lives aren't small, but you're living them in a small way. I'm speaking as plainly as I can and with great affection. Open up your lives. Live openly and expansively!" (2 Cor. 6:11–13 MSG).

We don't know exactly what he's responding to, but evidently there was something going on among the Christians at Corinth that he was compelled to address. Maybe he had heard some of them being petty and divisive. Or maybe he knew some of them had been offended by something and were turning inward with an unhealthy focus on themselves. One thing is for sure: He was appealing to them with great passion to not squander one moment on things that would pull them down. He didn't want them to waste the marvelous opportunity of life that the goodness of God has given them. Let's take a closer look at verses 11–12:

1. "I can't tell you how much I long for you to enter this wide-open, spacious life."

You can sense the urgency and excitement in Paul's words. It's as if he knows how easy it is for us to play it safe and miss out on the possibilities God has for us in our future. In my earlier book, *Good Things*, I tell the story of my visit to Snoqualmie Falls, a waterfall not far from where we live. It was discovered by settlers in the 1850s. At 268 feet, it's one of the tallest waterfalls in North America.[2]

That day, as we stood looking out at the water coming over the falls and into the river beneath, I felt like God put this word on my heart: *Kevin, the water you see cascading over the edge of the rocks is different water from the water that came over the falls this morning. It's not the same water that came over the falls yesterday, last month, last year, ten years ago, or fifty years ago. This water is new water, fresh water, water that has never been seen here before. That's how I want you to see my provision of blessing in your life. It's not the same blessing as yesterday, last year, or five years ago. I have a never-ending, ongoing supply of new favor, new opportunities, new territory, endless blessings that I'm bringing into your life.*

That moment has continued to encourage me to not settle with what was or what has been, but to look for and expect a consistent flow of good things to come into my life. Although the words are different, that's what this verse is telling us: God has more good things, more favor, more blessings in mind for us. Our job is to not get stuck where we are, but instead keep moving forward into the wide-open, spacious life He's given us.

2. "We didn't fence you in. The smallness you feel comes from within you."

Years ago, after Pastor John Osteen, Joel Osteen's father, passed away, my wife, Sheila, was invited to a small meeting that Dodie Osteen (wife to Pastor John) was hosting for pastors' wives. At that time, we didn't really know the Osteen family. We were not affiliated with any denomination and had been working hard to build the church God had called us to build. Our church was growing, and we had just moved into a bigger building, which meant that finances were tight, and we were using everything that came in and more to press forward. We didn't really have the extra resources to send Sheila to Texas, but we also knew that it was a great opportunity for Sheila to be with and learn from Pastor Dodie and other pastors' wives who would be there. So we found a way to send her.

On the day of the meeting, Sheila called me and said, "Kevin, I believe I'm supposed to give Dodie an offering. Is that okay?" Then she told me how much she wanted to give. I remember thinking, *Dodie doesn't really need an offering from us. I'm sure she's well taken care of. We're the ones who need an offering!* That was how I felt inside, but thankfully that's not what came out of my mouth. I knew that giving is not something we do only when there's a need. Giving is something we also do as a seed. I could tell Sheila was torn between our current situation and what she felt was an opportunity to sow a seed into the life of someone who had been such a huge blessing to so many people. I said, "Absolutely, do it!" Looking back, it wasn't that Dodie needed our gift. It was that we needed, in that season where we felt small, to not think small. We needed to realize that we were not fenced in and that generous giving was part of big living.

Remember, no matter what your circumstances are, don't let your own feelings of smallness fence you in. There will certainly be times in your life when your current condition will send you messages that will cause you to feel fenced in. Those thoughts that cause fear, worry, insecurity, and unforgiveness all come from within us. No one else has the power to fence you in or hold you back. Only you can do that to yourself, which is why only you have the God-given power to free yourself, to grow yourself. Only you can decide to get bigger on the inside.

> No matter what your circumstances are, don't let your own feeling of smallness fence you in.

3. "Your lives aren't small, but you're living them in a small way."

Most people who live life in a small way don't know how to live big. They are usually just following the patterns of those around them, especially their family and friends. Think about the generations of families who never go to college to get their education. Why would a family go generation after generation without going into higher education? Perhaps it's because of the limiting beliefs that get passed down from one generation to another. For example, it could be a belief that education is not important or that it's not affordable. Or it might be a belief that leaving home to go to college would be abandoning their responsibilities to their parents and siblings. These beliefs create limits on the family until eventually a son or daughter breaks free of the limiting beliefs. They enroll themselves in college and apply for grants and scholarships. They may work two or three jobs to get them through school. They stay up late; they take on full course loads. Then, graduation day comes and they get their diploma. Sometimes, it just takes one person in the family to change belief systems and start a new legacy.

When you live your life in a small way, you open yourself up to being jealous and envious of other people. You start comparing yourself to others in an attempt to overcome the smallness you feel about yourself. That leads to being envious when other people succeed. This is something that a lot of people (including me) have been guilty of. In fact, it's often the reason that people in the same company or the same church have trouble working together and succeeding as a team.

If we want to be all that we are meant to be, we have to be big and stay big on the inside. One way we do that is to be big enough to celebrate the success of others. When people around us get promoted, we have to make sure that we go big—we cheer on the people around us and refuse to let envy or strife have a place in us.

In the small church background I came from, there was an obvious bias against big churches. As a young man entering ministry, I was inspired by churches that were growing and reaching people in their city and region. Later on in life, I was doing my best, serving, giving, and working hard, but I could also see other pastor friends who were experiencing more progress and growth than we were. I started to at least understand how those small church leaders I had known as a young man felt the way they did. It's easy, if you allow yourself to feel resentful toward the success of others.

I've made a decision that with God's help I'll always fight against those feelings that would cause me to envy the success of others. I want to be big on the inside. I want to avoid comparing myself to others. I want to celebrate the success of those ahead of me and encourage the success of those around me. Most of all, I want to stay focused on being big on the inside, staying in my lane, running my race, and finishing strong. I'm thinking that you want to do the same thing.

It's helpful to consider the bigness of God and His perspective so that we don't get stuck in our own smallness. God's ways are greater than our ways, and God's thoughts are higher than our thoughts (see Isa. 55). Here are just seven examples of what God wants for us.

1. God wants us to see Him as a big, generous God.

This is so different from how most people see God. The enemy has succeeded with so many people in making God out to be small-minded, grumpy, and irritated by people who would be in pursuit of a bigger life. But the truth is that He wants good things for our life: To bless us and not to harm us. To give us a hope and a future (see Jer. 29:11).

2. God wants us to know He is not bothered by our fears and failures.

God is okay with your past failures. He's not interested in bringing them up or holding them against you. He also knows your struggle and fear in the present. But He wants to help you get past all of it. He wants you and me to overcome everything that would shrink us and put boundaries on us.

3. God wants us to live open, interactive, and engaged lives.

He wants us to be the most teachable and unoffendable people on the planet! He wants us to welcome council and guidance, to be secure in who we are in Him. To be easy to talk to about hard things. He wants us to encourage others and celebrate other people's strengths and progress.

4. God wants us to have big faith and big vision, and pray big prayers.

God told Abram in Genesis 13:14, "Lift up your eyes and look from the place where you are" (ESV). He told him that there was a vast land of opportunity in front of him. Just as He told Abram, He's telling you: See it, believe for it, and possess the land.

You've probably heard people say, "I'm just living for God in my own small way." Why not live for God in a big way? Whenever Jesus taught, he raised people's expectations of God's power and goodness in their lives. He encourages us to approach God with confidence that all things are possible and to have faith that He wants to give us good things.

5. God wants us to integrate into society to be "salt and light" in the world.

This means we grow and live bigger than a fault finder. Bigger than a critic. Bigger than a person who would condemn others. We grow up and get beyond the small talk of gossip and hearsay. An old saying goes, "Great minds discuss ideas; average minds discuss events; small minds discuss people." He wants us to bring life, hope, and help to the world instead of criticism, finger pointing, and accusation.

6. God wants us to grow relationally, emotionally, physically, spiritually, and financially.

Growing is a natural outworking of life. What if Amazon or Microsoft stopped thinking beyond this year's products? What if they said, "We don't see anything beyond here"? Of course, they would be out of business in no time. God has called us to live a life of ongoing, never-ending, generational progress.

7. God wants us to buy land, buildings, and occupy physical space.

One of the false things that religion has taught people is that getting rid of all worldly possessions is a sign of greater commitment and loyalty to God. But God doesn't want that. He wants his people to occupy land, own companies, build buildings, and have an increasing presence on the earth.

Heaven is looking for kingdom builders and legacy-minded people who occupy the earth on behalf of heaven.

Study Questions

1. What are forms of "fear" that you can identify in other people? See a list on page 67.
2. In what areas of your life have you built fences to protect you from hurts, rejection, or failure?
3. How can you begin to see and focus on God's bigness

instead of focusing on fear and feeling small on the inside?

4. Read over the seven things that God wants for us on pages 74–76. About which ones do you have the strongest faith? About which ones do you have the weakest faith?

CHAPTER 7

SAND AND STARS

When screenwriters and authors are looking for a story that can become a blockbuster movie or a best-selling novel, they look for a storyline that forms into a plot where a person or persons in the story are face-to-face with the odds stacked against them. When faced with the impossible, most surrender to the odds, unless a truth within them becomes more compelling than the truths around them. This is what happened around 2000 BC with a man named Abram and his wife, Sarai. They tried to have children for years but were unable to conceive. The fact that Sarai was barren was not the most unusual part of the story. Nor did that fact alone create the plot. The plot formed because Sarai's barrenness appeared to make impossible something that God had promised. God had told Abram that his children would be great in number and powerful in the earth. That promise, especially in those days, was a huge deal because it equated to an incredibly blessed and prosperous future. Many children meant many blessings. The greater the number, the greater your influence and credibility. The greater the number, the more referenced your name would be—meaning that you would be influential, prosperous, and powerful for hundreds, possibly even thousands, of years into the future.

The plot was formed with two opposing truths facing each other. One truth was a natural physical fact, that Sarai was barren. The other truth was based on the words that God said to Abram, "I will greatly bless you, and I will greatly multiply your seed as the stars of the heavens and as the sand which is on the seashore; and your seed shall possess the gate of their enemies" (Gen. 22:17 NASB). Abram had to choose to let God's truth in him be greater than what seemed like the truth around him. He had to believe in the sand and stars promise.

This is known as a simile, where you use figurative language, usually a word picture, to compare one thing to something different in order to emphasize or make something vivid and impressionable. For example, if you describe your daughter by saying, "She is brave like a lion," you are creating imagery to emphasize her bravery. If you say, "The news spread like wildfire," you are using imagery to emphasize how fast the news spread. While Sarai was barren, God used a sand and stars simile, a word picture to impress on Abram the vast number of children that were going to be born as his descendants. Talk about a mind-blowing experience! The imagery was meant to bust through the boundaries of Abram's mind, boundaries that had to do with his and Sarai's age and the facts around Sarai's barrenness. God wanted to open up Abram's mind to the bigness of his future. He wanted Abram to think big, way beyond the barren condition of his wife, to a vast number of children comparable to sand and stars!

Abram (who was later called Abraham) was growing on the inside for years. Every time he looked at the sand beneath him or at the stars above him, he grew a little bigger in his thoughts and confidence toward the future. Eventually Sarai became pregnant and a baby, whom they named Isaac, grew inside her womb. Not only did this promise come true in Abraham's natural genealogy, but add to that the religions of the world that refer to Abraham as the father of their faith, and the number is so high that counting the sand and stars was no exaggeration.

SEEING WHAT YOU DON'T SEE

Sand and stars are the biggest, deepest dreams you have for your future. There's no doubt about it, *sand and stars* can refer to something different in all of our lives. Even though the idea represents things unique to each of us, sand and stars happen when we start to imagine what we haven't seen. It grows stronger as we meditate on pictures in our mind that are the beginnings of something bigger and greater. Once that picture is in our minds, it starts influencing who we are, what we listen to, who we hang out with, what we sign up for, what we do with our money, and what we do with our time.

When we came to the Pacific Northwest, we had no money and only a handful of people who were for us, but I felt like I had a sand and stars promise. I saw a church full of life. A place of hope and encouragement where people could come to learn God's way of doing things. A place where broken people could be healed and lives could be transformed. A church where average people could become exceptional and could experience success in every area of life. I saw us reaching and serving thousands of people.

> ## Sand and stars are the biggest, deepest dreams you have for your future.

We've been serving the Greater Seattle-Tacoma area now for over thirty years. Thousands of people have said yes to Jesus, and thousands have been baptized in water. We have witnessed multiple generations of families growing up in our church whose grandkids are now on staff with our team! We're still walking out the sand and stars, but it's more and more a reality every day.

You may have a vision to own your own business, but you lack the resources needed to get it started—that's the sand and stars in your life. You may be hungry to help and serve a specific need that has become so evident to you that you're wondering why more isn't being done to meet that need. Yet right now you lack the education and credibility. You don't know how you can help or even if it's possible—that's your sand and stars. You may have family or friends who you are praying will surrender their lives to Christ. It could be a son or daughter. It could be your parents, a brother or sister, or someone you work with. You've invited them to church and said as much as you feel you can say, but they seem to have no desire to serve God. Their salvation is something you keep thinking about—that's your sand and stars.

It was twenty years before Isaac was born that God spoke to Abram and told him he was changing his name to Abraham. He told him then, "I have made you the father of many nations" (Gen. 17:5 AMPC). God referred to it as something he had already done. For Abraham it was twenty years of a sand and stars promise. Twenty years of looking up into the sky. Twenty years of holding grains of sand in his hand. Twenty years of getting bigger on the inside.

Sand and stars…Sand and stars…Sand and stars… Yes, it can mean something different for each one of us. It's those things we see in the form of a desire, a hope, a vision, a dream. Things that God puts in us that He wants for us in our future. "Now faith is confidence in what we hope for and assurance about what we do not see" (Heb. 11:1). It's what we see (in our mind) that we don't yet see (with our eyes).

Hold on to the picture in your mind. No matter how long it takes or how impossible it may seem, when God gives you a sand and stars kind of vision, He wants you to cultivate it and keep it growing inside of you until it becomes a reality.

Heaven-inspired vision is not limited to what might typically be thought of as being spiritual. It's not just prayer or Bible reading that causes sand and stars to become a reality. For Abraham and his wife, Sarah, it meant being pregnant for nine months, followed by sleepless nights, dirty diapers, crying babies, parenting, and providing for dozens of children and grandchildren. It meant navigating relational tension and family strife. They were not able to just buy a Winnebago with a bumper sticker that says, "I'm spending my children's inheritance." Sand and stars involved literally stretching them, causing them to grow on the inside and expand their territory beyond that of being nomads to becoming a large family enterprise.

The whole purpose of heaven-inspired vision is that it will become a physical reality. It will typically involve things like relationships, partnership, planning, team development, finances, land, buildings, education, strategies, organization, and structure.

Dave Ramsey graduated college with a degree in finance and real estate. As a real estate investor, he built a rental real estate portfolio worth more than $4 million. The bank that was financing his real estate was sold to a larger bank, which demanded immediate repayment on the loans. He was unable to pay and eventually filed bankruptcy. After recovering financially, Ramsey began counseling couples at his local church. He attended workshops and seminars on consumer financial problems. Ramsey developed a set of lessons and materials, and in 1992 he wrote his first book, *Financial Peace*, aimed at helping people to become debt-free. Ramsey's story began as a heaven-inspired vision and continues to change people's lives through Financial Peace University and other helpful resources. His sand and stars became a reality when it became an organization. Now it is hiring employees, purchasing land and buildings, and using media to continue its mission of equipping people to experience financial freedom. As often happens, Dave's sand and stars is helping millions of people to see their own sand and stars become a reality.

When people see themselves go from renting a home to owning a home, the first step might be to eliminate non-mortgage debt, free up their income, and otherwise position themselves to own a home. This is a step-by-step process. The process is held together and stays on track by seeing something they don't see. Most would probably prefer to have God just give them a house, but this is God's way of involving us and including us in the creative process. Seeing what you don't see is the beginning of the journey where an idea, a desire, a vision, a dream that's on the inside of you begins to become a reality.

> The whole purpose of heaven-inspired vision is that it will become a physical reality.

None of us is meant to simply observe what's going on around us, which is what so many people do. They notice the negative and then point it out as if there's a reward for seeing it. Some people protest and march with their friends down a street or on a college campus and go home feeling as if they have actually done something about the problem by noticing it and talking about it. Yes, observing is where we start, but we're not called to just see the negative; we're called to be the person God can use to create new and better realities. Most, if not all, of what God does on the earth He does through people, which is what *sand and stars* is all about. It's about a vision growing inside of a person and that person being a participant in the creative process, which means, to a large degree, that the works of God are subject to the willingness of man. Saint Augustine said it like this: "Without God we cannot, and without us God will not."

Scott Harrison was a twenty-eight-year-old top nightclub and party promoter in New York City. He organized parties for MTV, VH1, and major artists in the industry. There was a growing sense in him that there was more for him than the repetitious cycle of alcohol, drugs, models, and parties. He walked away from everything and began volunteering as a photojournalist for the Christian charity Mercy Ships, which had a fleet of hospital ships along the coast of Africa. During his two years with Mercy Ships, Harrison was exposed to the conditions of the impoverished in Liberia. As a response, he founded Charity: Water in 2006, a nonprofit organization that works to bring clean drinking water to people in developing nations. Beginning with no resources, Harrison, through his organization, has since raised over $300 million to bring clean drinking water to more than 8 million people around the globe.[1]

What's so amazing about the founding of Charity: Water is not just what it has accomplished (which is huge), but the courage it took for one guy to leave his successful career and become vulnerable to the possibility of falling flat on his face to do something so dramatically different than what he had done in the past. You can read more about Harrison's story in his book *Thirsty*.

God hasn't left you out. Everyone has sand and stars. There are things that God has planned for you that are intended to become a physical reality in the future. Right now, those things are only visible as a picture inside of you. It could be that God is waiting for you to open up your mind and expand your thoughts to accommodate what He wants to do through you. The process of sand and stars will always push you to grow bigger on the inside.

The reason God changed Abram's name to Abraham is because the name Abraham means father of many, and God needed Abram to start seeing himself not as he was but as he would be. In his current condition, Abram was not a father of any. But the plan was for Abraham to become the father of many. God wanted Abraham to see a bigger future every time someone called his name. Getting bigger on the inside wasn't just about seeing sand and stars, but also about growing himself as a father figure, a leader, a business owner. Getting bigger on the inside was an ongoing process for Abraham as he walked out God's plan for his life. He was challenged to grow by making bold decisions, creating alliances, settling disputes, and courageously leading his growing network and family forward. Part of his growth included a walk of faith that caused him to become the first person who received the gift of righteousness, or right standing with God, by faith in His promises.

> Don't doubt God's willingness to use you even though you may have past failures, present imperfections, or lack of education.

One of the most common things that God does is to use people who are unlikely candidates to become carriers of vision. There's a pattern in Scripture of God choosing unlikely candidates to bring heaven to earth:

- Esther was an orphaned Jewish girl in exile in Babylon. She became an advocate who saved her people from genocide.
- Moses was a foreigner in Egypt who had a speech impediment, but God used him to lead the people out of Egypt.
- The apostle Paul, the great church planter and writer of many books of the New Testament, was first a gang member who led the persecution of Christians.

We have all been given a "picture screen" on the inside where we can see things in our mind's eye that we can't see with our physical eye. This is how heaven comes to earth. Don't doubt God's willingness to use you even though you may have past failures, present imperfections, or lack of education.

Study Questions

1. What does the phrase "sand and stars" refer to?
2. Do you have a sand and stars dream in your heart? If so, what will it take to step out in faith? If not, start thinking of some dreams!
3. Does anything scare you about your sand and stars dreams?
4. What encourages you about hearing other people's sand and stars dreams come true?

CHAPTER 8

THINK 3

My grandfather, Roy Gerald Sr., was born and raised in Baton Rouge, Louisiana, with a family tree that had its share of bad apples. As a young man, he attended a tent revival, where he gave his life to Christ and never looked back. His life was radically changed and, as a result, so was mine.

My grandfather chose to walk the path God had for his life, which took our family in a whole different direction. God blessed him with continued promotions and investment growth as an employee of Exxon oil company. He was a consistent, committed, tithing member of his church. He volunteered as an usher, and he and my grandmother hosted the visiting preachers in their home. Before his life had an impact on mine, it first had an impact on my father. My dad grew up in that church, played his trombone in the church band, and was awarded high academic honors in school. But rather than continuing his education, he answered the call to ministry, loaded up the car Grandpa helped him buy, and headed to Bible college in Minnesota. Out of Bible school, my dad planted a church in St. Louis, where he pastored for over fifty years. What started in my grandfather continued in my dad and was passed on to me.

It was an unforgettable day for me when my dad brought my grandfather to visit my church, and the two of them sat with me in the front row of the church where I was now pastor. They attended all of the services that weekend. As the crowds gathered and people worshipped, I made sure that everyone there knew that none of this would have been possible for me if it had not been for the two of them. I am generation number three in my grandfather's legacy.

A LEGACY MINDSET

At the twenty-five-year mark of pastoring, I started to realize that the future of our church was going to be determined by how intentional we became about being a big-thinking, generational-minded church. As I wrestled with this growing sense of responsibility, it occurred to me how vital it was for us to be legacy minded. But then I wondered, *What does that really mean?* The word *legacy* seemed to be too general. I felt the need to be more specific so that we could be intentional. In the wrestling, I found inspiration around a concept that I call Think 3.

This concept helped me define what being legacy minded means to us. It provided clarity for me and gave me verbal handles with which I could communicate what I sensed God was saying to us as a church.

I realize that when you think legacy, you think future, but I felt like it would help if there was a well-defined goal. It dawned on me that when Scripture speaks of generations, it repeatedly references groupings of three. As I looked closer, it seemed to me that being legacy minded is to think at least three generations deep, beginning with your own generation, then your children's generation, and then your children's children. Make sure you don't skip over these next five verses; I think you'll find it fascinating, as I did when I first saw it.

Exodus 3:15: "The LORD, the God of your fathers— the God of Abraham, the God of Isaac and the God of Jacob."

Acts 2:17: "In the last days, God says, I will pour out my Spirit on all people. Your sons and daughters will prophesy, your young men will see visions, your old men will dream dreams."

1 John 2:13–14: "I am writing to you, fathers...I am writing to you, young men...I write to you, children."

Proverbs 13:22: "A good person leaves an inheritance to their children's children."

2 Timothy 1:5: "I am reminded of your sincere faith, which first lived in your grandmother Lois and in your mother Eunice and, I am persuaded, now lives in you also."

To abandon smallness is not just about thinking bigger; it's also about thinking long-term. Think beyond today, this month, or even this year. Christians call Abraham the father of our faith today, and it all started with a sand and stars vision. He lived with a vision that would outlive him.

I want to encourage you, no matter how young or old you are, to embrace this kind of vision in your life. So many people live day-to-day with no real thought of the future. But the families that leave the greatest legacy of power and influence are families that see beyond their lifetime to equip and empower future generations to go beyond where they have gone. Great families know that their children are their most valuable asset and greatest hope for the future.

> To abandon smallness is not just about thinking bigger; it's also about thinking long-term.

I was reading about Apple Inc. and how they host conferences and events for current and future tech developers. One of the feature stories describing these events told how Apple selected one hundred developers under eighteen to be part of their development process. One developer who has developed her own app for kids is only nine years old. The report said that these kids are part of the process of selecting what will and won't go to market.[1]

We could all learn from Apple! If they think generationally on behalf of their mission as a company, it makes all the more sense for us to think generationally on behalf of heaven's mission.

Think 3 is now at the core of everything we do at Champions Centre. It's a lot of fun because we are working a lot more with younger people, but there's also a sense of urgency in knowing that God's church, in this age of technology, has a very real and legitimate chance to impact the world. Scripture teaches us that God's plan for His church is that it would get stronger in every generation. I like to remind people that the church is God's plan A, and there is no plan B.

> Great families know that their children are their most valuable asset and greatest hope for the future.

If every generation of the church has to start over, you're not going to get any traction from one generation to the next. But if every generation can Think 3, then you start to have traction, and one generation builds on the works of another. To invest in future generations is the greatest investment that we can make.

This book highlights the courage of David, who was repeatedly vulnerable and put himself out there to live a life of purpose. He saw the future in a way that caused him to live with passion and invest himself over and over again to see the vision become a reality. In the process, God blessed David with wealth and fame, but David's ambition was always for the house of God. David loved and built the house of God. Reading the Psalms, you can't help but see it:

Psalm 26:8: "LORD, I love the house where you live, the place where your glory dwells."

Psalm 84:10: "Better is one day in your courts than a thousand elsewhere; I would rather be a doorkeeper in the house of my God than dwell in the tents of the wicked."

Psalm 122:1: "I rejoiced with those who said to me, 'Let us go to the house of the LORD.'"

Psalm 23:6: "Surely your goodness and love will follow me all the days of my life, and I will dwell in the house of the LORD forever."

In the same way that some people love and build universities, hospitals, and businesses, God's people are called to love and build the house of God from generation to generation. Perhaps the greatest and most selfless season of David's life was his last season. It was in that season that he championed a future that he would not live in. He showed us what it looks like to think big and think legacy, not just for his family but for God's church. Even though because he had been a warrior he was restricted from physically building the temple, he didn't leave the church or decide not to support the younger generation. No. Instead, he validated, he encouraged, he helped prepare and plan for God's house to be greater in the future than it had been in the past. He led in his giving and gave an over-the-top generous offering, estimated at over a billion dollars in today's economy, to see the house built. He then leveraged his voice on behalf of the next generation. Even though they were young and inexperienced, he fully supported them.

Live with vision that outlives you.

Here's some of the most heart revealing, unbridled words he spoke as he lived with a vision that would outlive him. "David said, 'My son Solomon is young and inexperienced, and the house to be built for the LORD should be of great magnificence and fame and splendor in the sight of all the nations. Therefore I will make preparations for it'" (1 Chron. 22:5). David may have been older, but he was still taking off the robe and dancing in the streets. He was still being big, selfless, and passionate.

Let me elaborate. David didn't say, "My son can't do this."

He said, "I'm going to do my part so that my son can do his part and together we can do something great for God! I see where I can help, and I see where the next generation needs me. This is not about me enjoying this new building; it's about a generational work that we can do together. We can build a house of great magnificence and fame and splendor that will impact the nations." That's exactly how it happened. The people gave, the leaders got behind it, and the vision became a reality because David lived with a vision that outlived him. You can have the same impact as David. Start living with a legacy mindset and see what God will do.

Study Questions

1. What does it mean to Think 3?
2. Have you recognized how often the Bible refers to multiple generations? What are some positive examples from the Bible? (Hint: Some are listed in this chapter for you.)
3. Have you experienced a positive legacy mindset of previous generations in your family or at your church? If so, how?
4. What are some ways you can invest and impact the generation coming after you?

PUSH PAST CRITICISM

"Any fool can criticize, complain, and condemn—and most fools do. But it takes character and self-control to be understanding and forgiving."

—Dale Carnegie

"There is only one way to avoid criticism: do nothing, say nothing, and be nothing."

—Aristotle

CHAPTER 9

COURAGE IN CRITICISM

David didn't seem to be surprised when Michal came to the entry of the palace and loosed her fury on him. You get the feeling that he already knew he wasn't going to get a welcome home party that night. It's as if he expected the criticism from her, which makes his decision to dance even more courageous.

The courage might have come from the fact that criticism wasn't new to David. He had critics all along the way. For example, his older brother Eliab spoke heavy, harsh criticism to David just before he stepped out to fight Goliath. Eliab accused him of abandoning his responsibilities at home. He told David to go back home where he belonged. Another time was at a place called Ziklag. While he and the fighting men were away, their enemy had invaded their outpost and taken all the women and children. On that day, his own men criticized him and blamed him for what had happened. What I want you to realize is that when David danced, he knew people would criticize. He danced anyway.

It's interesting how when you start to step out, the people closest to you can become your greatest critics. Sometimes people try to destroy you because they recognize your power and don't want it to exist. It's not that they don't see your strength; it's that they envy your strength.

David seemed to know that if he was going to live strong, he could not live safe. The only way he could live strong and lead strong was to risk exposure. He was not perfect, for sure, but from what we can see, he did not return criticism. He was like an old pro fighter sparring with a familiar opponent. Although criticism was familiar territory to David, it doesn't mean it was easy when he made the decision to dance. It just means he knew that the decision would cause some people to criticize him. His decisions always had.

Decisions always do.

THE STICKY FACTOR

As a young leader, one of my biggest regrets was that I read every letter of complaint and criticism that people wrote to me from beginning to end. As you read through this section, you'll understand why that has changed.

Like many people, I assumed that was what I was supposed to do: listen to everything someone wanted to say to me. By doing that, I thought I was proving that I was open to feedback and could take having people disagree with me. At that point, there were several things I hadn't considered. The biggest thing I was unaware of was the stickiness of criticism. Studies show that our wiring works against us when it comes to criticism. We're four times more likely to remember negative criticism than we are to remember praise. Nothing has a sticky factor like criticism. The rehearsing of criticism doesn't stop as we get older. Even when we know we shouldn't let it bother us, we stew over something or replay it over and over again in our minds. Our brains automatically process negative feedback more thoroughly than good feedback. You've experienced this at different times in your life, going back to your childhood when other kids made hurtful remarks about you or called you a name. That moment stuck with you and unsettled you. Sometimes those comments stick with us for the rest of our life.

Although some people have figured out how to handle it or dismiss common criticism faster, everyone has someone who, if they chose to criticize them, it would stick like super glue. Again, we are four times as likely to remember criticism than praise. In addition, psychology research shows that it takes our brain experiencing five positive events to make up for the psychological effect of just one negative event. This explains why many people are so thirsty for affirmation. The negative feedback in their life has far exceeded the positive. Usually, people who are in need of affirmation don't know it and have found a coping mechanism to help them survive the lack of affirmation.

Understanding the psychological and spiritual impact

criticism has on you is not about exempting yourself from criticism because it's too difficult to hear. No, it's about *qualifying and regulating the criticism* that you receive so that it serves you and makes you better.

QUALIFY AND REGULATE CRITICISM

Criticism is powerful, and anything that is powerful has to be qualified, regulated, and used properly or it becomes destructive. *To qualify* something is to make sure it's proven capable or fit for its use. When it comes to criticism, everyone is entitled to their opinion, but not everyone is *qualified* to criticize everything. If you're the one that's taking criticism, it helps to consider the source. *To regulate* something is to control or maintain the rate of speed so that it operates properly. When it comes to criticism, even if it's accurate, it's wise to regulate the amount of criticism you listen to.

After Sheila and I were both away from home, traveling, I came back ahead of her to an empty house. As I came in the door, I noticed an unusual odor in the house. It was late in the evening, and I was tired and ready to call it a day, so I grabbed something to drink, jumped in the shower, and got ready for bed. I thought a couple of times about the odor I smelled when I came in, but I couldn't really smell it anymore, so I went to bed and was lying there when something told me to get up and check around the house to see if I could figure out what I had smelled when I walked in the door.

After I looked around, everything seemed okay, but I decided to text a friend and ask what he knew about gas leaks. He texted me right back. We ended up getting on the phone, and he explained that I needed to go back outside for a bit and reenter my house to see if I could smell the odor again. I did that, and yes, it was strong the minute I walked in. He then told me to be careful not to turn on the stove but to look again and make sure that all of the knobs were off. As I looked at the knobs, my heart skipped three beats. One of the knobs was turned slightly in the on position. After turning it off, I went through the house opening windows and imagining how the story could have been different. Then I parked myself by a window, Googled gas leaks, and read more about how close I had been to going to heaven. I called my wife. I thanked God. There's nothing like a close call to remind you how blessed you are.

My point in telling you this story is to explain that criticism, like natural gas, has benefits for you, but only when it's used properly. When you live to make a difference, you'll be exposed to criticism. In the interest of your own calling and mission, it's important that you qualify and regulate the criticism you hear as much as possible.

Treat criticism like the powerful force that it is, knowing it can help you but can also hurt or even destroy you. It has the power, if it's unregulated, to push you off the streets and into the window, causing you to compromise who you are meant to be.

In some cases, I've been guilty of going to the window for self-preservation. In other instances, I've swung the other way, and even though I stayed in the streets, I got off mission using my energy to fight my critics. What I'm attempting to do now, that I hope can help you, is to accept and respect the effect criticism has on me. To know that I'm never completely immune to it and at the same time to not be afraid of it or controlled by it.

Fear of criticism will hold you in the window when you are meant to be in the street. In the same way that we regulate anything that's powerful, like natural gas or electricity, a healthy street life means regulating and qualifying criticism as much as possible.

CRITICS ARE NOT CREATED EQUAL

When you qualify your critics, you know that not all critics are created equal and that some shouldn't even get a seat at the table. We do people a disservice by telling them that they shouldn't listen to any criticism. The truth is that if you are fortunate enough to have people in your life who are qualified to critique you (more on this in chapter 10), those people's input is worth listening to even when it hurts to hear it.

When I talk about qualifying people, I'm referring to the fact that we have too many critics without credentials. Criticism to them is a hobby. It's something they like to do, but they're not qualified to do it at a level that's helpful to the people they criticize. An example of this is what football fans refer to as being an armchair quarterback, which refers to someone who doesn't participate in the game but still makes judgments about it. They sit in the bleachers or in their recliner and tell the coaches and the players what they're doing wrong. In reality, most of these armchair quarterbacks have never played or coached the game at a high level, but they sure do have an opinion on something they have little practical experience with.

A friend of mine recently retired from being an elementary school principal. He's spent his entire career in the classrooms and hallways of schools, solving problems, helping kids, and coaching teachers. He made decisions every day that impacted students, staff, and parents. He didn't presume to know it all and stayed proactive in learning and developing himself as a leader in education. What amazes me is the amount of time he had to spend hearing and responding to the criticism of parents who expressed their frustration about what they thought he and the rest of the school staff needed to do differently. He told me that as a father himself, he understood and always bent over backward to legitimize the concerns of the parents. He said that those people, even though their concerns came to him with a measure of criticism, were a joy to work with. What wore him down were the people who were mean-spirited, often angry, and inconsiderate and just needed a place to vent. He loved kids and education, but when he had an opportunity for early retirement, he took it because of the ongoing need to listen to and respond professionally to critics regardless of their attitude and credentials.

As I'm writing this book, there's a huge controversy over

whether we need a wall at the border of Mexico. I was in a gym exercising, and the TV tuned to a news program talking about the border wall. All of a sudden, the person exercising next to me started screaming obscenities at the TV. Even though I had AirPods in my ears, the volume of his screaming was way louder than what I was listening to. He was definitely not in favor of spending the taxpayers' money on a border wall. Then he turned to me and started soliciting my support for his angry opinion. It surprised me that even though he had never seen me before, he assumed I would be in complete agreement with him. Rather than responding like he thought I would, I asked him what kind of work he did. He said he had recently retired as the president of a major corporation in Canada. Then I asked, "Is Canada home?"

He said, "All my life."

I then asked if he had ever visited the border of Mexico or spent any time with the Border Patrol to understand what's actually going on at the border.

He said, "No, have you?"

I said, "Yes, I have."

At that point, it got quiet, he settled down, and we had a good conversation.

What was amazing to me was that he was a citizen of Canada, which means he would have paid his taxes in Canada. Also, he had never visited the crisis at the border and yet had a hostile opinion and profanity-laced criticism for the president and his plan for a border wall.

One of the things that helps me handle criticism is realizing that most of the time, the criticism I've experienced has had little or nothing to do with me. It also has little or nothing to do with facts. It has everything to do with the person doing the criticizing: their issues, their anger, their hurt. That's why we can't let the critics affect us or decide what we do. Our lives, our mission, our future are all too important to allow criticism to change our course.

It may surprise you (or not) that churches are not a safe zone from critics. In fact, churchgoing, religious people can be some of the meanest people in town. I heard recently from a man who was a pastor's son, had left church as soon as he was on his own, and had never returned. He said his journey away from church started when he was just a kid. He was scolded by an adult at church, who told him he was disrespectful for having his baseball cap on inside the church and told him to take it off. As inconsiderate as it sounds, if the truth were known, these unnecessary, hurtful comments happen more often than we realize. Great pastors and church leaders in towns and cities around the world live with constant disapproval from people who want their criticism to be heard. Christian artist Lauren Daigle was criticized by religious people for appearing on major television programs and award shows watched by millions of people. Pastors and Christian leaders all the way back to Billy Graham have taken criticism from religious people just for being at the table with our president and other political leaders. Joel Osteen wakes up every day to hate and criticism generated by judgmental religious people. It's always been this way. Jesus' biggest critics were the religious people of his day. Ultimately, they were the ones who got him crucified.

> Our lives, our mission, our future are all too important to allow criticism to change our course.

Doing your best and giving your all will not exempt you from criticism. If you are going to do something significant and meaningful with your life, you will experience your share of criticism.

AVOIDING CRITICISM

The mainstream media, talk shows on radio, and television now spend most of their airtime presenting news laced with various degrees of criticism. Cheap shots are common on late-night television, and drive-by assassins take aim by the minute on the internet. Follow the comments section on most websites and you'll find boatloads of hypercritical, cynical, rough comments and attacks.

Anywhere there's an opportunity to weigh in with an opinion, the comments are unfiltered and fierce. Without a bridle and free of hesitation, people are openly judgmental and critical of topics they know little about and, even worse, people they know nothing about. Criticism has more bandwidth than ever before, and it's not going away. We've all been criticized by someone for something at some time. No one is exempt from criticism, but it's dangerous to live your life attempting to avoid it.

Window logic concentrates on avoiding criticism. When you concentrate too much on avoiding criticism you become an overly cautious, compromised version of who you're meant to be. Aristotle said, "There is only one way to avoid criticism: do nothing, say nothing, and be nothing."

You'll still be criticized by somebody, because you can't please everybody. So, if living a life of purpose is important to you, you can save yourself a lot of internal struggle by deciding that your goal is not to avoid being criticized. That's way too small a goal for someone who wants their life to count. It's better and so much more rewarding to focus on being the best you can be and not worry too much about the critics.

Doing this takes more courage today than ever before. One of our staff whose job is to handle legal issues for our organization told me that he had been talking to our attorneys about what legal recourse there is for someone like me, as a pastor, or for us as an organization, when bloggers, reporters, or social media critics slander, attack, fabricate stories, and tell lies. The answer is that the threshold for slander is high for anyone who is a public figure. The higher the visibility, the less your ability to legally protect or defend yourself. Haters and critics can write pretty much whatever they want, true or false, without any consequences.

The reality is that the more good you attempt to do, the more vulnerable you will be to criticism. In regard to doing good, Eleanor Roosevelt said, "Do what you feel in your heart to be right—for you'll be criticized anyway." Jesus spoke of the certainty of criticism when he said that John and he were the targets of unavoidable criticism. Although they were deserving of respect, people still found something to criticize. He said, "John came neither eating nor drinking, and they say, 'He has a demon!' The Son of Man came eating and drinking, and they say, 'Here is a gluttonous man and a drunkard, a friend of tax collectors and sinners'" (Matt. 11:18–19).

One way to look at it is by realizing that if you're doing your best and being criticized, you are in good company with some great people. If Jesus, who was perfect, still had critics, then what chance do any of us have of not having critics? Even though criticism is not new, social media has given every critic a microphone, and the volume has gone way up. It's more essential than ever that anyone who is going to do life in the streets does not try to avoid being criticized.

What's worse than the criticism itself is the effect that criticism has on the people who hear it. The cause of the effect is usually unknown, because no one actually credits criticism as being the culprit. It just sounds too weak to admit, *I'm afraid of criticism.* But, even though it's under the radar for most people, the fear of criticism is having a greater effect on modern society than most people realize.

The best people with the greatest potential are choosing to avoid the criticism that comes with putting themselves out there, which then leaves the lesser-qualified in charge.

Talented, competent people who have a lot to offer are second-guessing whether they want to subject themselves to the scrutiny that goes along with the pursuit of their dreams. It's as if the fear of criticism has turned into a massive epidemic that is harder than ever to overcome.

People are playing it too safe by communicating a boring vanilla version of their ideas instead of taking aim at the extraordinary. People are holding back instead of contributing, in order to avoid having their ideas criticized.

- The fear of criticism is why people who have something to say don't speak up.
- The fear of criticism is why most people struggle to make decisions.
- The fear of criticism is why we're uncomfortable with vulnerability.
- The fear of criticism is why most people get defensive when other people offer helpful suggestions.

Listening to the never-ending sounds of criticism around you is making it more and more difficult to get past the fear that you won't measure up to expectations and will be judged severely as a result. Although this fear may not be a new phobia, there's no doubt that it's more widespread and common than ever before.

> Pushing past the fear of criticism starts by not trying to avoid it.

You can't help being aware of criticism, but there's a big difference between being aware of criticism and being controlled by criticism. But since the criticism is here to stay, the question is, what can we do to counter the negative impact it's having, which is causing some of the best and greatest people to look for a seat in the window?

Pushing past the fear of criticism starts by not trying to avoid it, by not changing our course when we know there's criticism ahead. If we can stop avoiding criticism, we'll end up where we are meant to be, living the life we are meant to live—in the streets, without the robe, and unafraid.

Study Questions

1. Think of an example of someone who uses their energy to fight the critics, or an example of someone who uses that energy to propel them forward. Which is more effective?
2. How is the fear of criticism currently holding you back?
3. Have you ever let criticism go to your heart?
4. How could you do better at blocking out the noise of a critic in your own life?
5. Consider the level of criticism you project onto others. What can you do to rein that in and assume the best about other people and situations?

CHAPTER 10

CRITICISM VERSUS CRITIQUE

My doctor was explaining to me the two different kinds of cholesterol. It turns out that one is LDL, which he said I could remember as the "lousy" cholesterol. The other is HDL, which is the "healthy" cholesterol. Both are cholesterol carried by two different types of lipoproteins. Like cholesterol, there's a lousy form of criticism and a healthy form of criticism. If you're going to live life in the streets, it's important to differentiate between the lousy and the healthy forms of criticism.

The healthy form is known as critique. The word *criticism* comes from the same root word as *critique*. Although *criticism* and *critique* originate from the same word, they are different. *Critique* is the method used by a *qualified* person who will observe someone or the work they do so that they can help them be better and do better. We all benefit from critique. When we listen to critique, it helps us identify our blind spots and see places we can get better. The Bible says it this way: "Listen to advice and accept discipline, and you'll be wise for the rest of your life" (Prov. 19:20 ISV).

So, while criticism can be lousy, even dangerous, critique can be incredibly healthy, even helpful. You can think of one as lousy criticism (LC) and the other as helpful critique (HC). The primary difference is in the carrier—the intent of the carrier, the words of the carrier, the spirit of the carrier. The LC is a person who is a critic, and the HC is someone who critiques. They are similar but different.

- Don't assume that HC will always be subtle and soft. Sometimes HC is direct and strong. In the same way, don't assume that LC will always be direct and strong. Sometimes LC will be soft and subtle.
- Don't assume that HC never stings or hurts when you hear it. It can sometimes feel like a slap on the face or a kick in the rear. If it hurts, it's a good hurt.
- There will be times in life where you'll have the opportunity to take LC and turn it into HC. This happens when the LC has an element of truth in it that you can use to make you better. Some mean people might deliver you a plate full of LC and walk away. Sometimes, none of it is true, and it needs to be thrown in your mental trash can. But sometimes you can find some meat on the bones before you throw it away.

Criticism versus Critique

Critics are self-appointed	Critique is invited
Criticism finds fault	Critique looks for ways to improve
Criticism condemns	Critique encourages
Criticism is an accuser	Critique is an ally
Criticism is designed to bring you down	Critique is designed to build you up
Criticism is opinionated	Critique is collaborative
Criticism complains	Critique considers
Criticism can be hurtful	Critique can be helpful
Criticism magnifies the negative	Critique magnifies the positive

Every accomplished athlete, on their way to greatness, has had to figure out the difference between LC and HC. They have to be able to tune in and listen attentively to a coach who is helping them while at the same time ignoring the voices of the critics in the media and in the bleachers. These athletes have some coaches who say it better than others, but it's always up to the athlete to hear the instruction and learn from it. Great athletes all pick up bad game habits along the way, and it's not unusual for an athlete to have to adjust a learned habit in the way they throw a ball, hit a ball, stand, or move their feet. A great coach can sound like they're picking the athlete apart when they are identifying a weak element in the athlete's game that needs correction. They might repeatedly bark instructions like "Get your head up…raise your right shoulder…put your weight on your back foot…keep your eye on the ball!"

All of this, even though it's direct and strong, is helpful critique. Nothing is more important for a developing athlete than their own coachability. When an athlete is in the early stages of development, they often get their feelings hurt by a coach who is trying to help them. Lots of young athletes have burst into tears or left the practice field after getting the download from a coach. An athlete may have incredible potential, but if they are not coachable, they're self-limiting. Another athlete may have less skill but go further because they're more coachable.

The same is true for us. We become the best version of who we're meant to be when we are coachable, eager to learn, and are open to correction and instruction. Scripture says, "Poverty and disgrace come to him who ignores instruction, but whoever heeds reproof is honored" (Prov. 13:18 ESV) and "He who hates reproof is stupid" (Prov. 12:1 ESV). That's what you call keeping it real!

What I'm calling critique is also referred to as critical thinking. Like critique, critical thinking is positive, helpful, and beneficial to anyone who wants to improve who they are and what they do. Although everyone thinks, much of our thinking, left to itself, is biased, distorted, uninformed, or downright prejudiced. Yet the quality of our life and what we produce, make, or build depends on the quality of our thoughts. When our thinking is distorted and biased, we lack the ability to identify what we can improve. Before a doctor can order a prescription, they must first accurately diagnose the condition of the patient. Critical thinking is analyzing and evaluating ourselves and our work while staying optimistic and proactive. Good critical thinking is what sets high standards and raises the bar of excellence in our lives.

We do our best in our organization to develop the critical-thinking skills of our leadership team. It's the main difference between a sloppy or average organization and an excellent one. At first, the most positive people on our team struggle to be critical thinkers, because it doesn't seem positive to them. They tend to shy away from seeing and talking about what's not working or how something or someone needs to improve. But once they experience the difference between critique and criticism, they become more comfortable with the process and become better at coaching others forward.

Those of us in leadership have a responsibility to create a culture where critical thinking is learned, encouraged, and welcomed by all members of the team. Sometimes critique will sting a bit, but this type of openness and vulnerability is essential for any individual or team to be their best.

No matter what your profession or calling, the people who reach their highest potential are always the ones who leave the window and become vulnerable in the streets.

There's no way around it. Steve Jobs said, "If you want to make a dent in the universe, you're going to take a few dents in your armor here and there." The same that was true for David when he danced is true for anyone who wants to make a difference in the world. Anything that attracts admiration also attracts criticism.

THE STARE DOWN

Sheila and I stepped onto an elevator. I hit the button, turned, and locked eyes with a guy who was already on the elevator. It was just the three of us, and for whatever reason, once our eyes met, neither of us looked away. As soon as we got off and the doors closed behind us, Sheila grabbed my arm, turned me toward her, and demanded to know, "What was that?"

I said, "What?"

She said, "You know what! That freaked me out! I don't know what you were doing, but don't ever do that again!"

After laughing so hard I couldn't take it anymore, I realized she wasn't going to let it go, so I explained that it can be a guy thing. There was something about the way he looked at me that caused me to feel like he wanted to send me a message, and it wasn't a Valentine card. My response might not have been the right one (especially if you ask my wife), but it was unplanned and happened automatically in the moment. I've got to admit that if he had been a big, muscular guy, my automated response might have been different.

Perhaps the most lethal effect of criticism on our life is that it can cause us to feel intimidated. The dictionary says that intimidation makes us timid (lacking courage and confidence), fills us with fear, and deters us from what we are doing. It comes to see if you'll flinch, squirm, get nervous, and cower in its presence. If that happens, it can be devastating to the plans and purpose God has for your life. Intimidation has caused a lot of people to back down and back away from the life they were meant to live.

The mentor, Paul, noticed that his younger protégé, Timothy, was intimidated and gave Timothy some great advice. He told him, "Don't let anyone look down on you because you are young" (1 Tim. 4:12). What he was telling him to do was to "stare back" at the look of intimidation when it comes your direction. Paul was saying, "Tim, stand your ground, go face-to-face, and don't back away from what you're meant to do because of what someone says to you or about you."

This could be the best advice the young leader ever received. If you're going to do life in the streets, you have to develop the confidence to be unintimidated by the stares and comments that are going to come your direction. When intimidation stares you in the face, stare back.

To be unintimidated doesn't mean to be arrogant. It doesn't mean you go looking for trouble. It doesn't mean you think you are better than anyone else, and it doesn't mean you're unteachable. It does mean, in the same way Timothy needed Paul to critique him, that we all need people who will coach and critique us. If you are intimidated by the critique, it will undermine the help that person can bring into your life. You want them to be direct. You want them to coach you forward. And that's not the only way being unintimidated will help you. On the flip side, being unintimidated means standing your ground and refusing to let the voice of criticism make you flinch. To be a strong leader, Timothy needed to be vulnerable and unintimidated by Paul's critique of him, while at the same time he needed to be unintimidated to be in the line of fire, making himself vulnerable to criticism.

THE SECRET SAUCE

Confidence is the healthy antidote to intimidation. It was David's secret sauce. He declared his confidence repeatedly in the Psalms. One example says this: "Though an army besiege me, my heart will not fear; though war break out against me, even then I will be confident" (Ps. 27:3).

> Confidence is the healthy antidote to intimidation.

What I like about this verse is that he's not pretending he won't have enemies or face adversity. He's not giving us a portrait of an unrealistic, easy-all-the-time kind of life. He's making it clear that life is a battlefield with real enemies and war zones. But he's determined that even then, in those times of challenge and adversity, he will remain confident.

Some people assume that when it comes to confidence,

you either have it or you don't. But what they don't realize is that confidence is like a muscle. You can build it and grow it. If your confidence is weak right now, it could be that it has not been exercised enough, and some time spent in the confidence gym could work wonders on your confidence. Being intentional in exercising and building your confidence will have a huge benefit on your ability to handle the critique you need and push past criticism you don't need to dwell on. Confidence is the secret sauce that separates the weak from the strong. It's the difference between those who make it and those who don't.

Maybe you're reading this and you would say, *Kevin, you don't know what I've been through. It's hard to have confidence after experiencing what I've been through in my life.* I want to encourage you, if you've been through a difficult season, that that's all the more reason to focus on building your confidence.

I love the way the writer in Scripture says, "So do not throw away your confidence; it will be richly rewarded" (Heb. 10:35). He's not only saying don't toss it aside. He's telling us that when we stay confident, it's only a matter of time before that confidence is rewarded. This is not just true for struggles we face. It's also true when we stay confident through the criticism that we experience from others. If you're the only one in your family serving God, chances are that you get hit with your share of opposition from the rest of your family. We have a lot of first-generation believers in our church, and I know what some of them have experienced from their family members who make comments, criticize them, and attempt to undermine their decision to follow Christ.

Sometimes you have to be quiet and not argue or defend yourself. You have to remember that your confidence is not just a positive-thinking strategy. Confidence is the greatest remedy for intimidation and is greatly rewarded. Everything you do in life, you do better with confidence. Confidence makes you a better Christian, a better husband or wife, and a better teammate at home, work, or church. Confidence helps you pray more often and more effectively because you believe in the power of prayer. When you pray confidently, you pray in faith that God hears and answers prayer. Confidence is central to an open, interactive street life. It makes you more comfortable in your own skin, and it makes you comfortable with others. The stronger your confidence, the more effective you are.

Study Questions

1. Take a look at the chart of criticism vs. critique (page 115). What surprises you in these comparisons?
2. What are some ways you can sharpen your critical thinking skills without getting overly critical?
3. Do you invite critique? If so, is it hard for you to accept it? If not, how can you open up and listen to quality critique?
4. How can you continue to build your own confidence to decipher the criticism or critique that comes your way?

CHAPTER 11

FILTERS

We were having problems with keeping our air conditioner blowing out cool air, so we had a company come out to inspect it. The repairman showed me the *very* dirty, junk-filled filter and gave me a college-level education on how an air-conditioning system works. As I listened to him, I remember thinking, *This guy has found his calling!* He was so passionate about getting his message across to homeowners like me to up our game when it comes to maintaining our air-conditioning system so that we maximize its performance. It was fun, because he was like a camp-meeting evangelist on a mission when he emphasized to me the importance of changing the filter on a regular basis. He said, "If you change the filter, everything works better! You cleanse the environment in your home, and you save yourself a lot of cost. If you don't change the filter, you're going to create problems for yourself. The air quality goes down, the equipment starts to malfunction, and it starts costing you more to live like you're living." I'm not typically interested in home maintenance (surprised?), but I love it when people are passionate about what they do, so I walked away inspired by the air-conditioning man!

Everyone has an internal filter. The mental filter was given to us by God to help us separate and process information and experiences that come into our lives every day. It was designed to filter out the stuff your soul needs protection from while allowing the good stuff to circulate in. When it's functioning as intended, it helps maintain a healthy perspective even in negative circumstances. But when the filter gets full of contaminates and is not changed often enough, it becomes the source of our problems rather than the protection it's meant to be. That filter holds in the junk, the bad experiences, the negativity, the disappointment, the rejection, the abuse. That's when people start circulating the wrong stuff into the environment around them. I'm sure you've seen this in people you've been around, whether it's at home, work, or church.

I was talking to a twenty-something woman recently who told me that she struggles with abandonment issues because all of the men in her life, including her father, have abandoned her. She's taking steps to overcome the guards she puts up and the mask she wears because she knows she can't have a healthy relationship with a man until she gets free of the contaminants that are part of her internal filtering process.

Scripture teaches us to be transformed by the renewing

of our minds (see Rom. 12:2). This is not meant to be a one-time or once-a-year thing but rather a consistent, daily part of our lives so that our minds stay unburdened and free.

People respond differently to the same circumstances. It's not that the facts are different; it's that the filter is different. The filter influences feelings, which influence actions, which is why the filter can work for us or against us—because all information and conversations, whether fact or fiction, get processed through your filter.

How you filter something determines how you feel about something.

- A filter can make you feel fear in the same situation where someone else feels brave.
- A filter may cause you to feel inadequate in the same circumstance where someone with less skill feels confident.
- A filter can cause you to feel offended when someone else feels thankful and appreciative.
- A filter can hold you back from an opportunity that someone else is eager to pursue.

The stickability factor in criticism heightens the need to filter criticism well. Some would refer to this process as "eat the meat, spit out the bones." It could be that there's an element of truth in what the critics say, and if you can stomach it, it's digestible and helpful. But there are also a lot of bones in criticism that are not digestible, words that you're not meant to have in your system. There's nothing good about those words—they are hard, they are not beneficial to you, and they can cause you to choke. The best thing for you to do is to quickly spit out the bones.

In some cases, everything the critic says should be filtered away from your soul and not allowed to linger inside you. It's all junk, based on the critic's lack of knowledge and poor judgment. In that case, there's nothing about it that is worth holding on to. Although you may emotionally have a need to process it with a trusted ally or two, after that don't think about it, talk about it, or waste any time or energy on it. Instead, concentrate on being confident, getting your focus back, and pressing forward.

FILTERING THE FLAWS

I had a friend growing up, Steve, who was born with the birth defect Amelia, and one of his arms was deformed. He used to say, "Anything you can do, I can do better." Amazingly, that was usually true. He was popular, made good grades, learned martial arts, was one of the best all-around athletes, and was the number one pitcher on the baseball team. His one arm was so strong that he threw the ball fast and incredibly accurately. Steve recognized his imperfections but maintained his self-confidence. He knew how to silence his inner critic and use the right filters to live fully free.

None of us is perfect. All of us have areas of incompetence and weakness. The way we filter the flaws and imperfections determines what kind of people we become. If you have to be perfect to approve of yourself, you'll never receive your own approval. Give yourself the same encouragement you give to people around you who you know are not perfect. When everything is filtered through an approval of yourself, you will live with assurance, joy, encouragement, and confidence.

The right filters factor in God's grace and thoughts toward us despite our flaws and imperfections. This was perhaps the greatest ingredient in David's ability to live the naked and unafraid life. At the core of his confidence, there was an assurance that he was a divine design. So, when others disapproved of him, he remained confident in himself, knowing that God approved of him. He praised and thanked God for how he was made: "I praise you because I am fearfully and wonderfully made; your works are wonderful, I know that full well" (Ps. 139:14). David knew he wasn't perfect. There are numerous times in Scripture where he talked about his flaws and prayed to God for help and forgiveness. His openness and vulnerability didn't weaken his confidence in himself. They actually made him stronger.

One of the main strategies of the inner critic is its disapproval of you. Knowing and reminding yourself that God approves of you is the best counterattack to the constant disapproval expressed by negative inner voices. Even though God may not approve of what you've done, He still approves of you!

Our tendency is to assume God approves of us the same way that people approve of us. We are so accustomed to gaining approval from our behavior and performance that we fall into the trap of approving of ourselves based on those standards. Since we don't typically measure up, we never really approve of ourselves. The better standard for self-approval is the unmerited, unearned approval of God.

Think of it like this: *Righteousness is* the gift of right standing with God. *Justified is* God seeing us just as if we had never sinned. The reality is that He already approves of you and me! We don't have to do anything to earn God's approval; the only thing we have to do is accept it.

Knowing that you have God's approval is such an important ingredient in living a truly free life. For some people, God's approval still isn't enough to quiet their inner critic, because the inner critic still works to undermine self-approval. It's like teenagers who feel confident in their parents' approval but still try desperately to gain peer approval. For some people, the assumption goes like this: God loves me because He made me and He has to love me, but I still don't look good, I don't fit in with most people, and I am average at best. When I do get opportunities, I always screw them up and say the most stupid things.

> We don't have to do anything to earn God's approval; the only thing we have to do is accept it.

If that sounds familiar, I want to suggest that you start speaking approval over your life. When you start *speaking* approval, it helps you to stop *seeking* approval. It creates an amazing shift that turns the tables on the inner critic, so that it is no longer leading the conversation into a search for approval because you know you already have it. Speak approval over yourself like David did when he said, "I am fearfully and wonderfully made" (Ps. 139:14). Speak the truth of being made in God's image, being born at the right time, and being in the right place. Speak with gratitude that you are blessed, strong, chosen, thankful, learning, growing, gaining ground, and getting better all the time. Speak the truth that you are loved by God, you are accepted by God, you matter to God, God is for you, and if God is for you, you win in all things and at all times.

The inner critic doesn't allow room for improvement, and it likes to tell you that you probably won't do better next time. You have to remind your inner critic that failure is never final. Remind your inner critic that as long as you're alive, there's hope of turning yesterday's failure into today's success.

> When you start *speaking* approval, it helps you to stop *seeking* approval.

You've probably seen the social media filters where you can use all sorts of images to distort your face, change the size of your head, put on dog ears or goofy glasses, and do all sorts of things to create various versions of your face. It's pretty crazy, and people have a lot of fun with it. What most people don't realize is that our self-image goes through our filters. I see myself through my filter, and you see yourself through your filter. The filter is where the inner critic is constantly trying to create a distorted, negative image inside of you that you then carry around with you.

Some people might say that the inner critic has actually helped them to succeed in life, pushing them to get good grades in school, get their degree, and be at the top in everything they do. But what happens more often than not is that the inner critic drifts into lousy criticism, tearing you down with talk that causes shame and unnecessary pressure and eventually undermines your ability to be the healthiest best version of you.

Stats tell us that most people have between fifty thousand and seventy thousand thoughts a day, and 70 percent of those thoughts are negative in nature. The nagging voice will tell us we're not good enough, we're not smart enough, we have no skills, we don't look good, we don't feel good, and we don't have enough discipline to change it. That same self-doubt might meet you at work and tell you, *You're under too much pressure. You'll never get everything done. No one even notices you. You should just give up.* That voice will speak up about our relationships and tell us, *They don't really love you. No one could care about you. It will never last. Don't kid yourself. Don't be stupid. Don't be vulnerable.*

Rather than being emotionally and spiritually free, you

become a slave to the relentless voice of shame and con-demnation that tears you down rather than builds you up.

Some days you might have to change the filter several times so that you can have a fresh, untarnished attitude. There is a formula I've used to renew the spirit of my mind, which I talk about in more detail in my book *Mind Monsters*.[1] I call it FAITH:

Focus on the positive.
Affirm yourself.
Imagine God doing something good.
Trust God in everything.
Hope for the best.

I first scribbled this acronym on a piece of paper at a point when my internal dialogue needed to change. I memorized it, and now it's my go-to when my filter is full of the wrong stuff and the inner critic needs to be put in its place. This acronym is what I use to interrupt the negative internal di-alogue and redirect it positively. The idea is to tell yourself these five things. And as you do, these things will happen that are necessary for renewing your mind: You'll bring fo-cus back to the positive things in your life. You will affirm yourself. You will move your thoughts toward faith in God. Trust and hope will rise within you.

Of course, you don't have to use this formula, but I rec-ommend that you have a dependable go-to for continually renewing the spirit of your mind. The mind is no different from the air-conditioning filter that serves you well and then has to be replaced. You need to continually cleanse and refresh the parts of your mind that tend to hold on and get filled with various forms of negativity.

Life in the streets means falling down, messing up, getting criticized, and feeling hurt. It often leads to us second-guessing ourselves, our decisions, and even our potential to go forward. What starts off as *I am enough* can become *Am I really enough?* This change in our perspective is known as cognitive distortion. It's a mental filter that changes our perspective from one of confidence to one of self-doubt. We begin to question ourselves, our strengths, and our potential. We start to embellish our fears, magnify our flaws, and exaggerate our weakness. Our mental filters start to pick up limiting, unhealthy distortions that have to do with ourselves, and we start to see ourselves differently from how God sees us. To reverse the effect of the negativity, the contaminated filter has to be changed so we can recapture a fresh mental and spiritual attitude. In Ephesians 4:23 (AMP) it says, "and be *continually* renewed in the spirit of your mind [having a fresh, untarnished mental and spiritual attitude]."

In the same way the air-conditioning man showed me the old filter and said I needed to change it often, this verse says *continually* be renewed in the spirit of your mind. *Continually* means every day and even several times a day, depending on what kind of day you're having.

"SHAME OFF YOU"

Shame was what Michal tried to put on David after he danced in the streets. He didn't accept it. Shame is sometimes called the "master emotion," meaning that it's like having all the other negative emotions wrapped up in one. It's the feeling that we're not worthy, competent, or good—that we're, in a sense, rotten at the core. While guilt says, "I did something bad," shame says, "I am bad." The inner critic justifies beating us up internally to save us from the embarrassment of underperforming at home, school, work, or church. Shame causes us to confuse who we are with what we've done.

Sometimes the message is *Shame on you if you don't work really, really, really hard.* Or, *Shame on you if you're not tougher, smarter, and better than the other person.* If you were raised going to church, the "shame on you" message may have even become the primary filter through which you came to know God. If so, your perspective of God is now associated with feelings of shame instead of a sense of acceptance, grace, and love. If this is true for you, then that's a filter you're going to want to change. The "shame on you" filter is not part of God's message for your life. Jesus did not come to earth and die on a cross for us to carry our own shame. He came to carry our guilt and shame so that we don't have to carry it. The redemptive message of the cross is a "shame off you" message!

If you're feeling shame in your life, it's not going to produce anything but guilt and condemnation. The Bible says,

"There is no condemnation for those who are in Christ Jesus" (Rom. 8:1). You might need to put this verse in as the new filter through which you process your sin, mistakes, and failures. Rather than holding on to a filter that is filling your life with shame, get a "shame off me" filter and start seeing yourself the way God sees you. God doesn't define you based on weakness and imperfection. He has defined you through the finished work of the cross, which is our hope of salvation.

The wide-open, all-in approach to life leaves plenty of opportunities to second-guess yourself. You make the decision to dance knowing that you open yourself up to be booed by the critics and targeted by the haters. You also know that you're going to make your share of mistakes along the way.

David faced extreme blame and shame at Ziklag. He and his men returned from battle to find that their enemies had plundered their small city and taken all the women and children captive. The emotions escalated as warriors screamed in agony and wept uncontrollably. David himself crumpled to the dirt, overwhelmed by the deep despair that could be likened to being emotionally ripped apart. After they wept until they could weep no more, the men began to talk of killing David with stones. Somehow, even with the blame aimed at him and the shame he felt for letting this happen, David started to filter out the blame and the shame and started to encourage himself.

I've wondered what that might have sounded like. He had no Apple AirPods to slip on and no worship set to play loudly in his ears. Did it start as a whisper talking to himself? Did it start with the familiar lyrics of a song? There's no way to know, but one thing is for sure: On the worst day of his life, David must have drawn on past victories for encouragement. He must have brought to mind God's faithfulness, because he was able to filter the tragedy through his own words of encouragement. He was able to encourage himself in the Lord. David had his share of courageous moments, but the resolve he showed in pushing past the criticism that was around him and within him that day was courage at its highest level. And yes, he got them all back—every child, every wife, every woman who had been taken. David and his men recovered them all.

Maybe you've sat too long in the aftermath of a tragedy in your life. Perhaps it's time to apply the filter of God's promises so that you can get on the road to recovering everything the enemy stole from you. Maybe it's time for you to encourage yourself in the Lord, to remind yourself that He's still with you and for you.

QUALIFY THE POSITIVE

When my grandson Kyan was a bit younger, we would go out in the yard to hit golf balls. He might have ten good hits on the ball, but then if he had a few bad hits, he would start saying things like "I'm not good at golf...I can't hit the ball," and he would give up trying. If it was basketball, he would say the same thing. He would do really well, and then when he messed up or missed some shots, he would suddenly go from being Steph Curry to being a loser. He magnified the bad and forgot the good. Of course, the goal was and still is to keep him swinging or shooting until he had that swag back and felt like a champion again.

I came across some research that described how most of us, when we're children, learn how to "disqualify the positive." Children who do this find ways to explain why positive experiences don't count.

- If they're not making good grades and a teacher reaches out with concern to help them, the child sees it as insincere. They reason that if the teacher really wanted to help, he or she would give them a good grade.
- When a parent, teacher, or coach enforces a rule or discipline, a child often interprets it as "Everyone is out to get me."
- When a child who has been left out is included, they often see it as someone just being nice. The belief that's already in their mind is that people don't really want them on the team, at the party, in the group.

The study said that even though we may mature in some ways, even as adults, it's common for us to keep disqualifying the positive in life. As I read the research, I thought, *This is familiar. It's definitely something I've done.* I remembered when I played sports that I could have a strong game and do a lot of things well, but it was the strikeout or the fumble that I took home with me and let haunt me. I remember disqualifying the hits I got, the touchdown I scored, or the leadership part I played on my team.

Even now, my natural tendency is to disqualify the positive feedback or encouragement I get from many people and focus on what a critic said or what I failed to do as well as I could have. Chances are that you have this same tendency to disqualify the positive, especially when it comes to yourself. The critic in you is constantly seeing what you do wrong, and you're failing to give yourself enough credit for what you do right. For example, when your best friend, your mom, or your husband says positive things about you, maybe you think, *They just say that because they're my friend.* Or when you sit down with your boss and in the same conversation he tells you some things he wants to see you improve in and says some good things that he sees in you or appreciates about you, do you hear what needs improvement but dismiss the compliment assuming, *My boss is just trying to be nice*?

Your inner critic has two predictable strategies: constantly exaggerate the negative and disqualify the positive. If allowed, the critic within you will point out all your failures and none of your success. It will tear you down if you let it. But you have the final word.

Study Questions

1. What does an internal filter do when it's functioning like God intended versus when it's contaminated?
2. Discuss or think of a time when someone you know disqualified the positive.

3. What is your go-to thought process? Do you need to make any adjustments?
4. What are some of the lies you have believed from your inner critic that you need to replace? What are some of God's truths you can replace them with?
5. If you feel like you are in a pattern of shame, what is one commitment you're willing to make to start changing that pattern in your life?
6. Look again at the acronym FAITH on page 131. What letter stands out to you the most in this season of your life?

CHAPTER 12

DON'T COME DOWN

The book of Nehemiah is the story of Nehemiah, a man who God called to return to his homeland and rebuild the walls of Jerusalem because they were in ruins. As the story unfolds, you start to realize that Nehemiah was an exceptional leader who, though he had the favor of God and man on his life, had to deal with the relentless, nagging voice of critics.

One of the best examples of how he handled his critics is found in the exchange that occurred between Nehemiah and three critics named Sanballat, Tobiah, and Geshem. The critics were officials from neighboring cities who were envious of Nehemiah's success. Word of his progress started to spread, and they kept hearing how great of a job Nehemiah was doing in rebuilding Jerusalem, which was something they didn't want. Maybe they felt threatened by it, or it made them look bad, but whatever the reason, they launched a media campaign to try to undermine the credibility of Nehemiah. In the sixth chapter the critics sent word requesting Nehemiah to come and meet with them. Nehemiah knew they were scheming to hurt him, so he sent messengers back saying, "I'm doing a great work; I can't come down. Why should the work come to a standstill just so I can come down to see you?" (Neh. 6:2–3 MSG)

They came back four times, and four times he replied the same way. The fifth time, they changed their strategy from distraction to intimidation. They sent an unsealed letter making up a story about Nehemiah having a secret agenda and threatened to expose him. But Nehemiah stood his ground and refused to give in. They became more and more determined to unsettle him, but he wouldn't flinch. They hired people to lie about him, but he stayed focused. Then they hired people to tell him that he was going to die if he didn't stop building the wall, but Nehemiah knew they were not voices that he should give any time or attention to. He knew they were trying to undermine his confidence and take him away from the work God had called him to do.

This is a great example to us that all critics are not equal. Not everyone who wants us to listen to them deserves to be heard. Some critics are sent to distract you, intimidate you, and take you away from the places that deserve your time and attention.

When you're doing a great work, don't come down.

When complainers call, don't come down.

When critics talk, don't come down.

When lies get told, don't come down.

When distractions beckon you away, don't come down.

I think everyone who experiences criticism feels pressure to talk to the critics, to hear them out and to respond to them. There can also be a temptation to defend ourselves to the critics. But just because that's what people want us to do, or think we should do, doesn't mean it's the right thing to do. Oftentimes the right thing to do is what Nehemiah did—don't respond to a critic. Criticism doesn't usually deserve a response. If an ally, a teammate, a coach, a leader, or a trusted friend is questioning you, then by all means, make sure you are open to their council and input in your life. The people who have your best interest in mind deserve a response from you. The critic, however, can be a distraction from the things that are deserving of your time and attention. When that happens, you lose focus on what matters most and end up exhausting your energy explaining yourself or defending yourself to your critics.

Another thing that we can learn from Nehemiah is that he wasn't reliant on the approval of others to feel good about himself and the work that he was doing. Notice he said, "I'm doing a great work..." Nehemiah's critics had told him that the walls he was building were not going to be stable and strong. They mocked and called his work inferior. But Nehemiah remained confident in the work God had given him to do. Whether it's raising children, building a business, serving as a missionary, writing songs, providing clean water to a remote village, helping in your child's classroom, or leading in a life-giving church, when you're doing what you're called to do, don't let the voices of distraction pull you away from your assignment. Don't let the voices of discouragement diminish your work. When it feels futile or pointless remind yourself, "I'm doing a great work; I can't come down."

Don't let people who want your attention on petty issues that arise make you feel guilty as you stay focused on great things. By the way, the great work is not always your career or your ministry. Sometimes that great work involves taking care of your family, spending time with your kids, and doing what you need to do to stay healthy and consistent in the things that God would have you do.

In Nehemiah's case, after just fifty-two days, the walls were finished, and Scripture says the surrounding cities and nations rejoiced, giving God glory for the work that was done.

MAKE IT FUN

What Nehemiah did next was a surprise. He ordered a mandatory time of fun and feasting. Remember he is one of the greatest leaders in the Bible who, starting with low morale and no finances, somehow led one of the most successful building projects in history. The reason I'm emphasizing that is so many people assume they have to choose between hard work and having fun. They have bought into the idea that fun is a waste of time and hinders productivity.

That great leaders can't risk being playful. But research shows the opposite is true. Research shows that if people are dropping their guard and having more fun, they will work harder, stay longer, maintain composure, get along better, have more unity, which all translates into greater accomplishments and a more meaningful life. Nehemiah said to the people he led, "This day is holy...Do not mourn or weep...Do not grieve, for the joy of the Lord is your strength" (Neh. 8:9–10).

In most people's minds, even today, holiness is not equated with fun. Holiness is seen as being sad, somber, reverent. In many churches and religions, fun is considered frivolous and even sacrilegious. Nehemiah says the opposite. He basically rallies people to make room for fun and says, "This day is holy to the Lord so no long faces, no sadness, no weeping, no grieving. Only joy." He's not asking if they *feel* like having fun. He's not asking if they are in the *mood* to celebrate. He is telling them to choose joy because the joy of the Lord is your strength!

Have you noticed that some of the most meaningful things we do in life can be a drudgery and a burden unless we decide to make them fun? Things like education, working, raising kids, saving money, owning a home, serving God, or going to church can become a burden we bear or a blessing we enjoy. None of these things are fun unless we decide to make them fun! You do yourself a favor when you decide to have joy in the journey. I don't know about you but this is something I've had to work at, and one of the verses of Scripture that has helped me is Ecclesiastes

8:15 (NLT), "So I recommend having fun, because there is nothing better...for people in this world than to eat, drink, and enjoy life."

- Nothing better for a person than having fun.
- Nothing better for a marriage than having fun.
- Nothing better for a home or family than having fun.
- Nothing better for a team, a business, or a church than having fun.

"That way they [you] will experience some happiness along with all the hard work God gives them [you] under the sun."

Whether you are building a wall, facing your critics, or doing what matters most in your life, here are three courageous habits than can make what you do more fun:

1. Generosity on your face.

My youngest grandson, Kody, is a fun, loving, singing, dancing, joy-filled three-year-old. Recently, he was being hurried along by his mom, who had her hands full and was pulling him as she carried some things to the car. She was in a rush to leave and as she quickly put him in his car seat he looked her in the eye and said to her, "Mom put your fun face on!"

I think this is so funny, because if you're like me, putting on your fun face doesn't happen on its own. My tendency is to get trapped in my head and unaware of what's on my face. Recently, I was on a plane and when asked if I wanted to eat, I listened to what was offered and said I'd just wait and eat later. After a while the stewardess returned and offered me a complaint form to fill out. She said she could tell I wasn't very happy. Evidently my face was not very generous and she was surprised to hear that I actually had no complaints and was on my newest favorite airline! As I told her this with a big smile on my face I realized that I had not smiled since I got on the plane—and it felt good to put my fun face on! Generosity begins on our face. It helps others and it helps us. As often as you can generate a generous face, do it. That simple act of courage will add joy to your journey.

2. Levity in your heart.

The word *levity* comes from a Latin word for "lightness." Jesus said, "My yoke is easy and my burden is light." Want to add joy to the journey? Want to have a healthy life? Better relationships? Have the courage to lighten up. To laugh at yourself. To maintain levity when you feel heaviness and retain lightness under pressure. By doing this you fuel friendships and strengthen relationships. Nobody wants to be around anyone who is heavy-hearted and burdened by life. On the other hand, everyone enjoys being with people who maintain levity in life. Have you ever said or heard someone say after a good laugh "I needed that!"? That's a reference to the fact that lightness and joy make life more bearable. Ella Wheeler Wilcox's poem "Solitude" says it so well: "Laugh and the world laughs with you; Weep and you weep alone."

My wife Sheila has attention deficit disorder. Early on in our marriage she would get so upset at herself that it put added stress on our relationship. She would move things constantly...not just her things, but my things. Which makes sense when you know that her idea of marriage is that my things are her things and her things are her things. (Yes, I'm trying not to laugh out loud as I write this because it's funny how true it is!)

To deal with her frustration, she did two things: First, she developed some helpful habits that I'm sure she would be glad to share if you asked her. Second, she started laughing at herself when she couldn't find something and knew she had put it somewhere. It could be my stuff or hers, but she would always announce it like this, "We're playing hide and seek again ...whoever finds it wins!" Sometimes there would be a prize for the winner, usually the kind that only husbands and wives can imagine. I'm really proud of her and the decision she made. She could have kept getting upset and down on herself. That began years ago and to this day, it's amazing how often levity lifts us up and keeps us from giving in to our frustrations.

3. Praise in your mouth.

I'm grateful for the popular surge in worship music. There are so many talented writers and artists today that are giving voice to the worship that is in the heart of all who are grateful for God's unfailing, unconditional love. Praise is different than worship. Praise is the joyful noise. Praise is fun, festive, and celebrative. Praise makes you want to break out the moves and do a little dance. Praise is especially potent in helping us have joy in the journey. Praise displaces heaviness, elevates the goodness of God, and celebrates life. "The garment of praise is for the spirit of heaviness" (Isa. 61:3, NKJV).

The reality is that life is hard. The other reality is that God is good. If you want to keep your balance in a slippery world that tries to bring you down to its level of discouragement and defeat, add more praise. Learn the vocabulary of praise until you speak it fluently and habitually. Often and with ease. Praise is a powerful antidote to self-criticism and the criticism of others.

Before I move on, let me ask you to consider making these three things a formula for having more fun while you live a committed and meaningful life. Add joy to your journey by sharing this with others and making it a daily habit of self-proclamation.

I have:

- Generosity on my face
- Levity in my heart
- Praise in my mouth

PROVE THEM WRONG

Some would say that Tiger Woods is the greatest golfer of all time. I'll leave that debate to people who know more than I do. Whether he's the greatest golfer or not, he is definitely the king of the comeback. When he won the Masters Tournament in 2019, it was the fifth time he'd won the green jacket. But what was most amazing was that it had been eleven years since Tiger had won his last major championship. Shortly after that, his career, his life, his marriage, and his health took a downward turn. He went through personal setbacks and made some bad decisions, as well as having several back surgeries. Even though he continued to play, everyone thought he was done. The golf analysts had repeatedly weighed in with their opinions that he would never be able to compete with the best golfers again. They said his career was over and he was done.

Here are just a few of the things that were said:

- "Tiger Woods's long, slow decline has been painful (for him) and tedious (for us). His fourth back surgery, announced on Thursday, has added a sense of finality: It's over. He's done."
- "I do think we'll see him in PGA Tour fields from time to time, starting in 2018, but his days as a threat to win are over."
- "Never say he'll never play again. But also don't look for him to win."
- "I'm afraid this is the end of the road. Yes, we need to celebrate the glorious golf Tiger played, but it's also OK to feel a little cheated. Tiger is the most dominant golfer of all time, and also the biggest what-if."
- "Wanting him to return [as a player] at this point is

wanting to see him suffer in real time. I'm not sure I want to be a party to that torture any longer."

- "Woods's balky back would prevent him from ever being competitive again."
- "The mental side of the game, the loss of the so-called 'edge,' is as much of a hurdle for Tiger as the injuries. Yes. His competitive drive and confidence were incomparable in his prime. But that swaggering Tiger is no more, and I don't see him coming back."[1]

These comments all came from different experts on the game of golf, and this list represents only a sample of what was the widespread commentary. This doesn't mean the analysts are bad people or didn't have the right to their opinion. Analysts are not the same as reporters. They are not expected to report only the facts. They are also at liberty to have conversations and make predictions based on those facts. When you understand that, you begin to realize that Tiger at forty-two years old not only had physical challenges to overcome but he also had the mental challenge of knowing that people who had made a career of making accurate predictions were predicting that he would never play well enough again to win a major.

Then Tiger did the unthinkable. On April 14, 2019, he pushed past the criticism and won his eighty-first PGA Tour event!

We all love it when someone stays determined and eventually perseveres to prove the critics wrong, because we know that the people who get criticized are the people who, at the very least, had the courage to be in the streets. Even if they don't finish the wall or win the tournament, we know they deserve to be celebrated for not heading to the safe place where the more timid, frightened people stay when they fear what critics might say.

There's no way to be sure, but I have a hunch that Nehemiah used the criticism as fuel to motivate him to prove the critics wrong. The important thing is that he stayed the course and completed his assignment while not reacting to the critics or letting them get him down. To finish the wall in fifty-two days was a remarkable feat that could be done only by highly motivated, skilled workers.

Like Nehemiah, you and I have an assignment. When we face opposition and criticism, we don't have to get discouraged or quit. We can make the same choice that he made. The choice to stay focused, relentless, and determined to persevere in the assignment God has given us to do.

Study Questions

1. What do you like most about Nehemiah's response to his critics?
2. How can you apply the tenacity that Nehemiah and his people had to your own dreams and desires?
3. What does the phrase "don't come down" mean to you after reading this chapter?
4. How can you add joy to your journey?

OWN YOUR STORY

"The moment you accept responsibility for everything in your life is the moment you gain the power to change anything in your life."

—Hal Elrod

"We should be too big to take offense, and too noble to give it."

—Abraham Lincoln

"If you never heal from what hurt you, you'll bleed on people who didn't cut you."

—Anonymous

CHAPTER 13

THE POWER OF A PATTERN

This section is about taking complete ownership of your life. Not just the things that you are responsible for but for everything that impacts your life. It's about taking ownership of the cards you were dealt and the pain you have felt so that you, with God's help, can create a positive outcome. Only when we own something can we determine its influence on us. The best leaders and the most successful people are the ones who cast no blame and make no excuses. Rather than a pattern of complaining or finger pointing, these people have developed patterns that cause them to be proactive, solution-oriented problem solvers. They own the outcome for everything that is influencing their life, even those things that were unavoidable and circumstances that were beyond their control.

Pain is part of life. It's inevitable. But what's more debilitating than the pain itself is the pattern the pain creates. The logic of the window is formed by the pain experienced in the streets, which explains why Michal was in the window. She didn't become a window-watcher on her own. Window logic was what she heard. It was the reasoning of the house she grew up in. It was the pattern passed down to her by her father. She grew up in the house of Saul, an insecure and troubled king who had become small on the inside—irrational, guarded, worried, suspicious, threatened, and desperate to maintain his position of power.

The former king had started off much like David, a brave warrior who fought for the freedom of his people after the threats of a dictator named Nahash the Ammonite. Unfortunately, the journey that he began in courage had shifted to one driven by fear. In his early days of leadership, King Saul was popular with the people and was open and receptive to the mentoring guidance of Samuel. However, just about the time David came on the scene, we start to see King Saul becoming distant and isolated. His fears started to dominate, causing him to be emotionally unstable. He became an insecure leader who adopted the logic of the window as his pattern of survival.

So, imagine Michal growing up in that atmosphere, hearing her father talk about not trusting anyone. Imagine her listening when he was irritable and had fits of anger, taking his rage out on the people around him. He had been her hero, but he soon became a narcissistic maniac, rejecting the advice of Samuel and trusting his own irrational logic.

Rather than accepting ownership he adopted a victim mindset. He saw others as the problem, which is why killing David eventually became his obsession. When you are a mad king, everyone bows to your pattern of behavior, even if it's a pattern of pain. When you're the daughter of a mad king, his pain causes you pain, and your pain creates its own pattern. You withdraw, sit in windows, become critical, and blow up with rage when your husband dances in the streets. It doesn't mean you're evil. It means you're hurt and broken.

HEALING THE HEART

We all experience different kinds of heartbreak throughout our lives. In fact, an enormous number of people today are broken, injured, disabled, and hurting on the inside. This is what the Bible calls the "brokenhearted."

The word *heart* in Scripture is a reference to our entire inner being. It's our mind, soul, and spirit. So when Scripture talks about the brokenhearted, it not only applies to people who are mourning the loss of a relationship or a loved one. It's broader than that. The word *brokenhearted* applies to everyone who has been hurt and is hurting on the inside.

One of the significant keys to living the life you are meant to live is knowing that just because you've been hurt, it doesn't mean you have to stay hurt.

Why do I say that? Because God has created you to heal. Remember childhood cuts and scrapes? They turned into scabs, and even though some of them may be scars today, your body healed itself. In the same way God created you to heal physically, He also created you to heal emotionally and spiritually. But the only way back to wellness is a habit that's counterintuitive. It may seem unreasonable, but when you respond to hurt with faith and confidence, you will experience healing for every kind of hurt.

> Just because you've been hurt, it doesn't mean you have to stay hurt.

Whether God's healing is predetermined or in response to your prayers for supernatural intervention, it all comes from Him. He heals you emotionally, physically, and spiritually. Jesus came to heal the brokenhearted and set the captives free (see Luke 4:18). This doesn't mean that you won't have to go through a process or put yourself out there to receive support from friends and counselors, but it does mean that God is on your side and will heal your broken heart.

God doesn't want any of us to live from a place of past pain. He wants all of us to experience wellness and wholeness in every area of our lives. That only happens when we exercise the privilege of deciding our response to whatever hurts, offenses, and injustices we face.

It's your story, and you alone have author privileges. No one gets to decide your response except you. When it comes to your story, God has given you the privilege to determine how the chapters unfold. When an unwelcome, difficult chapter comes into your life, only you get to decide if it is just a chapter or the story of your life. Some people make the mistake of taking a bad chapter and making it the story of their life. You don't have to do that with your story. Instead, you can say, "This is my story, and a bad chapter doesn't define me. God is my strength, my help, my healer. Although I may have had a setback, my story is going to be about a comeback. I may have had an experience where I felt offended, but I refuse to live offended. I may have been hurt, but I don't have to stay hurt. I may have been rejected, but I live from the reality that I'm accepted. I may have experienced hate, but thank God I know I am loved."

Part of being vulnerable is having the courage to own all of your story. If you're a teenager driving your parents' car and it stalls on the side of the road, you might shift responsibility and say, "It's not my car; it's my parents'. I don't have any money, so it's not my problem." You could call your parents, and they would take responsibility for the problem. On the other hand, if you're an adult and your car stalls, you may not like it, you may not know what caused it, and you may not be a good mechanic, but it's your car. It's up to you to get it off the side of the road, pay to get it towed, pay for the repairs, and get the car going again.

People who don't think like owners will always live calculated lives, measuring their time, energy, and investment. They never want to invest more than the minimum to get what they want. The problem with this is that they will always underestimate what it looks like to give their best to the people and the opportunities God gives them. At the same time, successful people own what is theirs. Their pride of ownership doesn't stop with their personal property. They think like owners.

- In their neighborhood: They call it "my neighborhood."
- At their place of employment: They call it "my company."
- At the church they attend: They call it "my church."

Owning your story means you don't just own the good parts of your story; you own every part of your story. You own the good, the bad, the mistakes, the sin, the pain, what you can control, and what was out of your control. It all becomes part of your story.

> Owning your story means you don't just own the good parts of your story; you own every part of your story.

I have a friend who got caught up in an extramarital affair. When it all came to light, his wife was devastated, heartbroken, and angry. He felt so ashamed and had deep regret. He loved his wife and asked her to forgive him. They decided to try to fight for their marriage. The path of healing is not easy. When you've been betrayed at that level, you have to fight hard to overcome the feelings of betrayal and regret. You have to fight hard to navigate the questions and accusations that keep coming up. Forgiveness is not a one-time thing. It has to be on repeat. It's a choice you have to make over and over again. The good news is that this couple owned the crisis, moved past the blame, and did the hard work of accepting the infidelity as part of their story. Today, years later, that couple's relationship is restored and healed. They laugh, love, and serve in God's house.

PATTERNS OF PAIN

There's a story of a rancher who owned a bunch of horses. One day he noticed one of the horses had kicked the wood fence and scraped his leg badly in the process. So the rancher and his helpers cleaned the wound and bandaged the animal's leg. A few weeks later he noticed that the horse was still bothered by that bruise, and so he asked the veterinarian to come and have a look at the horse. After the veterinarian examined him, he gave the horse some antibiotics and the horse got better for a few days. But as soon as the antibiotics were gone, the owner noticed that the leg swelled up more than ever and was worse than before. So he called the vet, the vet came back, and after looking at the horse, the vet said, "I'm going to have to look deeper here."

He put the horse under anesthesia, and once he got deep enough he discovered a large sliver of wood that had gone far beneath the skin when the horse had hit the fence months before. They had been treating the symptoms rather than the source of the horse's pain.

The same kind of thing can happen to us. We run into fences, get banged up a bit, and end up with a lingering wound that stays with us underneath the surface of our life.

When this happens, it causes us to be more guarded and suspicious of others, especially anyone who shows interest or tries to get too close.

Owning the pain means owning the pattern of the pain. A pattern of pain might cause a woman who was hurt by a man in her past to be cynical and suspicious of all men, which means her past relationship will always have a negative effect on her current relationships. For the hurt person, the pattern is one of survival that protects them from experiencing more relational wounds in the future. What they fail to see is that the pattern of their pain makes it difficult—if not impossible—for healthy people to be a part of their lives.

Amy and Donna met each other at church and were starting to develop a friendship, when Donna told Amy that she didn't want to be friends anymore. After a few weeks, out of concern, Amy texted Donna and said, "Hey, no need to answer. I just wanted to say I hope you're doing well." Donna answered right back and said, "I'm so excited to hear from you! I didn't mean what I said about not wanting to be your friend. I just wanted to see if I mattered enough for you to come after me."

Talk about drama! This is what unhealed past relational pain can look like. The hurt person thinks it's okay for them to say hurtful things and walk away, and if the other person doesn't come after them, then that other person is the one at fault. This logic is twisted, which is always the case when it's a product of pain. The reason this sort of twisted logic doesn't work on healthy people is because healthy people don't respond to manipulation. Hurt people often use manipulation and other tactics out of their own place of fear and insecurity. They may not realize they are doing it because it's become a normal part of their approach in relationships. The result is zero chance of them having relationships with healthy people unless the manipulator gets healed. Healthy people will be kind to them, consider them, possibly even want the best for them, but the only close relationships a person who is fenced in by fear can have are relationships with people who are inside the same fence living in a pattern of pain.

Donna's issue was that she was afraid. She was held back from the life that God had for her because of the fear inside of her. These kinds of fears are very common in our society today. In fact, it's easier to find people with unhealed hurt that translates into fear than it is to find people living free.

Window logic based in fear and self-preservation denies you your power to love like you've never been hurt, play like you've never had pain, sing like nobody's listening, and run like you've never fallen down. It doesn't give you a better life. It holds you back and causes you to miss the better life.

You don't have to let yesterday's pain determine today's behavior. You can stand up to the impulse, go against the pattern, and reset rather than react. Put your energy and faith to work, knowing you are an overcomer and God is your healer.

> You don't have to let yesterday's pain determine today's behavior.

A great couple in our church, Alan and Kate, had a miscarriage and lost their baby at fourteen weeks. Shortly after that, a friend of Kate's was having a baby shower. Even though she knew it wouldn't be easy, Kate went to the shower with a big smile and celebrated her friend's baby. We heard about her courage from a woman who was there and told us how inspired she was by Kate's unselfish, generous, and brave actions that day. She said there were tender moments when Kate shed tears and felt waves of emotion, but the fact that she was there and in good spirits inspired the women around her.

I think we would all agree that it's so encouraging to see people who don't shrink back when trouble comes knocking on the door or when heartache comes into the living room of their life. There are a lot of people who wouldn't have gone to a baby shower that close to the loss of their own baby, and we all would have said that we understood. Some would have spent a lot of time asking questions there are no answers to. We all go through things that hurt and cause pain on the inside, things like rejection, abuse, abandonment, betrayal, divorce, the loss of people you love, severed relationships, disappointing setbacks, and financial setbacks. Just because you've been hurt, it doesn't mean you have to stay hurt. Every time you're hurt, you can be healed.

We have to get the word out. Too many good people with great potential for their future are stuck in the idea that their past has stolen their future. Your history doesn't determine your destiny. You don't have to let the pain of your past destroy the hope of your future.

We all have a tendency when we're going through these kinds of things to assume that our pain is unique to us, that others don't know how it feels. Especially when we look around and see people who are blessed, happy, and healthy while we are struggling, hurting, and trying to survive. When you look at those people, it's easy to assume that they have never been hurt like you have. There's no way they could have had any experiences similar to yours and be doing as well as they are.

The truth is, everyone has a story of struggle. Everyone has suffered heartache and pain. The difference is that some people assume that "once hurt means always hurt," while others know that pain is unavoidable but staying hurt is optional.

Jesus went to Jerusalem for a Jewish holiday. As he was making his way through a crowded section near the pool of Bethesda, there was a man who had been an invalid for thirty-eight years. He was brought to the pool, where he would lie on a mat until someone would come and carry him home. "When Jesus saw him lying there and learned that he had been in this condition or pattern for a long time, he asked him, 'Do you want to get well?'" (John 5:6).

I think it's safe to assume that Jesus asked that question based on the fact that getting well would require the man to change a pattern he had become comfortable with. If he was healed, he would not be carried. If he was healed, he would have less support from others. If he was healed, he would be able to go to the fields and work. If he was healed, he would have to be brave. He would have to do things he'd never done before. He would have to be intentional and mindful to develop new patterns. Jesus started this by telling the man to do something he had never done before. Jesus said to him "Get up." To disrupt the pattern of pain, Jesus introduced a pattern of healing.

THE PATTERN TO YOUR HEALING

Just like there's a pattern to your pain, there's also a pattern to your healing. The path of healing begins when we choose the path of a person who is healing.

The pattern of healing for the lame man in Bethesda meant doing the complete opposite of what he had been doing for thirty-eight years. The question to consider about this moment at Bethesda is what came first: the movement or the miracle? Was he healed while he lay on the mat, or was he healed moment by moment as he moved? I think it's safe to assume that his new life began as he moved. Not before he moved, but as he moved. This is how we heal from our past pain. We don't get healed *before* we move; we get healed *as* we move. We start to experience something we haven't had as we do something we haven't done.

Don't wait until you are strong to move as if you are strong.

I've experienced several broken bones, but when I broke my hip, it required more therapy than other injuries I've had. The therapist explained to me that the therapy was not primarily about the injury to the bone. The bone was healing without therapy. The therapy was about me doing what I could do, which was strengthening the muscles that bear the weight, while giving time for the broken bone to heal.

My movement, even though it made me uncomfortable, was contributing in a major way to the process of healing. I remember feeling afraid to move. Afraid I wasn't able to move like they were telling me to move. Also afraid that if I moved, I would injure myself again.

In that short time after the injury, I had embraced my broken condition with all of its limitations as my reality. The pain was dictating my behavior. This is what brokenness and pain do. They take over, telling you what to think, what to do, what to say, and how to act.

Using my experience as an example, think of it this way: God heals the bone, but our movement plays a crucial part in our complete healing. Trust God that as you move, He heals. He does what only He can do while we do what only we can do. He heals the broken as we get up.

If you keep doing what you've been doing, you will keep getting what you've been getting. In the same way that Jesus was disruptive to the patterns in this man's life, he wants to disrupt the pattern that pain has created in your life.

Charles is a longtime member of our church, a fun-loving guy who was by his wife's side as she battled various forms of physical illness for many years. A couple of years ago we said goodbye to her and celebrated her life in the month of December. Charles is a gifted actor and had for years played the part of Scrooge in our production of *Scrooge: The Musical*. It just so happened that in that year we were taking a break from doing the production. *Scrooge* is a festive, fun, and extremely popular holiday event in our city, seen by tens of thousands of people.

A year later, as we prepared for the holiday season, Charles was dealing with the fact that he had lost his wife the previous December and had decided to not be involved. We have other people who also play the part of Scrooge, so I knew we would be okay to do the musical without him. But I also knew that this was something that had meant a lot to Charles, so I decided to reach out to him and ask him to reconsider. I explained that it would not only be a way of him bringing joy to others but also a path of healing for him. I said that even though he felt emotionally better staying on the sidelines, serving from his place of pain could be part of his healing. And to his credit, that's what he did.

I watched as he pushed himself and poured himself into the performances. During the holidays he thanked me for reaching out to him and encouraging him to go against the lingering emotional pain that was holding him in a negative pattern. He shared with me how liberating and refreshing it was for him to be involved. That's what it looks like to fight for freedom.

PAIN WILL ALWAYS CHANGE YOU—BUT ONLY YOU CAN DECIDE HOW IT'S GOING TO CHANGE YOU

Pain gives bad advice. Past pain will tell you to step away when you should actually step forward. Pain will tell you that you don't need anyone, but the truth is that two are better than one. It can begin with something simple like not making the team or not being in the inner circle at school. After experiencing rejection, you find that pain wants to start dictating your actions. When it does, rather than walking in confidence, you become timid and afraid.

As part of your story, you will go through difficult experiences in your life, and those experiences will never leave you like they found you. The experience drops you off at an intersection, and only you get to decide which direction you'll go. Why? Because it's your story! This is when it's most important to know that you are not a victim of your circumstances. You are not a bystander in your life. You are not an observer. You are the writer. Where the story goes from here is up to you.

You can take bitter street or better street. You can choose to be hurt, or you can choose healing. You can walk in fear, or you can walk by faith. When some people experience pain, they get a chip on their shoulder, and others come out with an attitude of thanking God. Some people get weaker under pressure, and other people get stronger.

When I see people who are unjaded, joyful, and optimistic, I often wonder what they had to go through on their way to joy. When I have a chance, I ask some of them about their story and what they've faced in life. It always amazes me how deep wounds in their past now only have a scar. The pain is past, maybe with a bit of sensitivity when they talk about it, but they have experienced healing from the hurt and moved on to experience a blessed life. God never promised us that we wouldn't have heartache and pain, but He promised to be with us in all of it and to heal us every time we experience hurt.

Study Questions

1. Discuss or reflect on this quote: "Pain is unavoidable, but staying hurt is optional."
2. What are some identifiers of "patterns of pain" in relationships?
3. If you're going through a tough season right now, what are some ways you can make sure this is just a chapter of your story instead of the rest of your story?
4. How can you begin to take more ownership of all of your story?
5. Just like there are patterns of pain, there are also patterns of healing. What are some patterns of healing you practice in your life? Or, what are some patterns you want to begin to implement in your life?

CHAPTER 14

UNOFFENDABLE

I stared at the psalm thinking that I would see a clause, an exception to explain what seemed to be impossible. It felt for a moment that I was reading the bio of a superhero rather than a human being. A Marvel comic, not the Bible. But that's what it says, "nothing shall offend them." Real people with real emotions have the power to be unoffendable. "Great peace have they which love thy law: and nothing shall offend them" (Ps. 119:165 KJV). *Maybe this is it,* I thought. *Maybe this is the main thing that created safety for David in his vulnerability.*

If *nothing* is a scandal, a snare, or a stumbling block. If *nothing* holds me in hurt or stirs me to strife. If I have no quarrel with anything God does and no issue with what others say, then maybe my heart stays free and I stay open to live and love like I've never been hurt, which would then mean that being unoffendable has to be the common pursuit of all who dare to dance.

When I was a kid, my parents had a container filled with Bible verses. Once a week we would reach in and pull out a card, not knowing what it said until we picked it. The idea was that we would memorize the verse that week and be rewarded for it. Of course, I always hoped for the shortest verse.

The writings of Psalm 119 are like a container of 176 verses that are mostly disconnected from each other, as if they are snippets from David's journal compiled later in life and brought together to become the longest psalm. It's likely that David told himself this one thing over and over again to keep himself focused and free: "Great peace have they which love thy law: and nothing shall offend them." David was far from perfect in this category but relentless in his pursuit. What makes it even more potent is that this proclamation was written in the aftermath of his own justified reasons for being offended. Just to name a few:

- When Samuel the prophet came looking for a leader, David's father excluded David from the lineup of potential candidates. He was overlooked and underestimated.
- When David was considering going to battle with Goliath, his older brother accused him of arrogance, belittled him, and told him to go home.
- When his popularity grew with the people, King Saul, the authority figure in his life, became jealous and made numerous attempts to kill him.

Like David, we all have opportunities to be offended—reasonable opportunities. On top of that, we live in a highly sensitive, easily offended culture where it's trendy to be offended. In our society, being offended is seen as being brave. If you're offended, you have a chance of being a hero. If you're not offended, today's culture tells you that you should be. Not only should you be offended, but you should let people know you're offended. Hashtag speakout, anyone? But the truth is, anybody can be offended. What takes real courage is to remain unoffended. While some people look for opportunities to be offended, God calls us to live unoffended lives. To pursue the place where *nothing* has us in the grip of offense. If you're wondering how you can be unoffendable, I promise I'll get there, but let's first look at some reasons why you don't want to be offended.

FIVE REASONS NOT TO BE OFFENDED

1. *It's exhausting.* It takes a lot out of you mentally, physically, and emotionally. Offense triggers emotions of anxiety, anger, and strife. Some vent on social media, others spill their emotions on friends or family, and others churn under the surface, hashing and rehashing the offense. The body and mind go into overdrive, which causes stress, robs you of your peace, makes you restless, and disrupts your sleep—causing you to be indifferent and irritable. Its sounds like an oxymoron to say "fight

for peace," but that's exactly what you're doing when you repeatedly resist letting your mind dwell on an offense. God keeps us in perfect peace when we keep our minds trusting in Him (see Isa. 26:3).

2. *It's distracting.* It takes the focus off of the things that matter most and consumes your attention with things that should really matter less. Whatever consumes your mind controls your life. Every time someone rants on social media, TV, or talk radio, you've got to wonder how much better their life would be if they used their time and energy to create memories with their kids or volunteer for their church or serve a cause in the community. The life God has for us is found when we stay focused on good things and resist the distractions that pull us away from the things that matter most.

> Whatever consumes your mind controls your life.

3. *It creates collateral damage.* If you live offended, it will spill over into your kids, your marriage, your work, your ministry, and your relationship with God. One of the most common stories I hear when I'm talking to people who went to church as a kid but stopped going is that something happened at church that upset their mom and dad, so they quit going and haven't been back. Huge rewards and generational blessings happen when people free themselves from the trap of offense. If you want

the best for your family and future, keep freeing yourself from offense.

4. *You attract other offended people into your life.* Offended people are attracted to each other. Offense becomes a common ground where they start to build an alliance with people who are also distracted and creating their own collateral damage. They typically refer to each other as best friends because they justify each other's wrong choices, validate wrong feelings, and ultimately hinder each other from getting free of the offense or growing in Godliness. Proverbs 22:24–25 (ESV) says, "Make no friendship with a man given to anger…lest you learn his ways and entangle yourself in a snare."

5. *Healthy people will start to avoid you.* Living offended will cause the healthiest people to avoid getting too close to you. People who want to be free of offense and live positive lives will realize that they can't do that with you. When this plays out in real life, offended people often assume that the people avoiding them think they are better than them. The reality is that healthy people recognize offended people and understand the risk of breathing in secondhand smoke. The best thing you can offer other people is a healthy you. An offense-free you is a gift to yourself, your spouse, family, church family, the people you work with, and those you come in contact with every day.

THE TWO STAGES OF OFFENSE

Everyone's story includes feelings of offense. Things that offend people are unavoidable. Jesus said, "Offenses will come" (Luke 17:1 KJV). He told his disciples that "All ye shall be offended because of me this night" (Matt. 26:13 KJV). So, no matter who you are, where you come from, or what your background is, things that offend people are going to happen to you. This is not something you can control. And when it happens, it doesn't mean you did anything to deserve it. It just means that you're like a soldier engaged in battle. When you sign up to live a meaningful life, you willingly risk injury, including friendly fire. Jesus' words were absolute and inclusive to all of us who live a life of purpose. *Offenses will come*... How they come and when they come is uncertain, but the fact that offense comes is inevitable.

The first stage of offense is *feeling* **offended.**

It's possible that you have felt offended this week or even today. Something someone did or said caused you to feel overlooked, insulted, taken advantage of, or not considered. The feeling of offense is when someone presents you with an opportunity to be offended. It's like they pour you a big glass of straight-up offense and serve it to you. It can be a stranger, a person you work or go to school or church with, or someone you live in the house with. It can be a friend, your boss, a team member, a coworker, a team leader, the pastor, your kids' teacher, or the self-appointed church cop. It usually happens quickly and without warning. There it is, like a glass of cold water being handed to a thirsty man, the glass of offense is poured and served to you. You hold it in your hand. You stare at it. Try to make sense of it. You might even ask some friends to look at it and tell you what they think. Was it fair? Is it justified? How could someone serve you treatment that you don't deserve?

The feeling is not something you can always control. For some who are already living offended, it's a feeling they've carried throughout their life, which has caused them to be more sensitive than others. But even for those who are less inclined to feel offended, it's not something you can always avoid. Everyone feels offended in some way, at some time. When you feel offended, that's when you have to start fighting to not be offended. Living offended starts with feeling offended.

The feeling stage is the place where you have to stand your ground and fight for the *great peace* in your life that can be found in God's word. When you proclaim God's promises, just like David did, you experience God's great peace. Like a seasoned fighter, you develop the ability to take a punch, but that doesn't mean you don't feel it. It's in stage one that you have a choice to make: *Do I drink the cup of offense or not?*

> When you feel offended, that's when you have to start fighting to not be offended.

If you didn't know you had a choice, don't feel bad. For years, I didn't either. Most people don't. But whether you knew it or not, you do have a choice when you feel offended to not live offended. Just because you are served an offense, feel the offense, and stare at the offense, it doesn't mean you have to drink the offense.

The second stage of offense is *living* offended.

This is like drinking poison and expecting the other person to die. To live offended is to live hurt, self-centered, bitter, envious, or angry. Living offended is a way of abdicating ownership of your life versus maintaining ownership. Owning your own story can be hard, but it's not nearly as hard as spending your life enslaved by your story. Being vulnerable is risky, but it's not nearly as dangerous as letting bad experiences take over and call the shots. Offense is a dictator of attitudes and behavior. Once it pushes itself into position, it rules both mind and spirit. Under the rulership of offense, context is contaminated and perspective is polluted. If you listen carefully when the offended person talks, the offense has managed to integrate into every part of their life. Like a virus on a computer, it has spread throughout their life and is impacting the way they see things, hear things, and respond to things. They blame, make excuses, withdraw, disconnect, disrupt, and live defensively. This doesn't mean they are bad people. Good people often drink poison and unknowingly abdicate ownership to the dictator named offense. Everything about their life is filtered through the offense. The only way for them to be free is to stop empowering the offense and start taking ownership of their story.

DON'T DRINK THE POISON

Have I told you I hate snakes? I hate snakes. But because I love the outdoors, I've run into a few of them, which is too many. The most memorable snake sighting happened when we were on a safari in South Africa. My wife was seated behind me in a high jeep easing down a dirt path. We had just seen some lions on a zebra kill and were easing down the dirt road looking for other South African game. All of a sudden, what looked like a rope flying through the air came within a few feet of our heads. The next fifteen minutes turned into a chaotic standoff between our guides and a nine-foot-long black mamba. Due to its aggressive nature, its tail that acts like a spring and gives it the ability to "fly" through the air, and its fast-acting venom, the mamba is the deadliest snake on the planet. In most cases, people die within minutes of being bitten, and without antivenom, the fatality rate from a black mamba bite is 100 percent.

Obviously, it was a really close call for us, but the next thing that happened was something I didn't expect. The four people who lived and worked on that property went after the snake with no weapons except rocks and big sticks they used like clubs. I asked later why they didn't just leave the snake and let us get out of there. They said that as part of their community, if they see a black mamba, it's their duty to kill it. To let it live today would mean that one of them might die tomorrow.

The extent to which those men went to protect themselves, their friends, and their family from being poisoned has stuck with me. Poison is not meant to be in our system. When we are physically poisoned, it damages our nervous system and vital organs and can end our life. When feeling offended turns into living offended, it has the same kind of consequences to our spirit as drinking poison has to our body. God has a better plan for us, a plan of ownership in our story. It's a plan that accepts every part of our story as our story of God's never-ending, ongoing purpose in our lives. Owning it all means that we see all things working together for our good. We have no one to hate, no one to blame, and no one to accuse. If every time we feel offended we stay the course and remain intentional in grace, openness, honesty, and forgiveness, the offense will have no power over us.

When John the Baptist was in prison for preaching, he started feeling offended that he was there. "Why hasn't Jesus come for me? Why am I the one in prison and Jesus is free?" John sent some of his followers to question Jesus, and Jesus told them to tell John, "Blessed is the one who is not offended by me" (Matt. 11:6 ESV). Jesus knew that John was feeling offended, and this was his way of saying, *Don't drink the poison.* The blessed life, the healthiest life, the most productive life is the life that is free of offense. Owning your story doesn't mean you won't feel offended. It doesn't mean you won't get served a big glass of offense. What it means is that since your story is your story, you have the privilege to pour it out. No one can offend you without your permission. No one can keep you rising above what is done and said. When Jesus says, "Blessed is the one who is not offended by me," he's differentiating between living with offense versus living free of offense. The outcome of your life is not the same. Not even close. When you own your story, you exercise your power to choose.

> Owning it all means that we see all things working together for our good. We have no one to hate, no one to blame, and no one to accuse.

In the movie *The Family Man*, Nicolas Cage plays a character named Jack. We get to see the difference one choice makes in Jack's life. We see how it plays out differently if he gets married to the love of his life versus not getting married and pursuing a high-powered career.[1] If you've seen the movie, you know how differently it plays out. If not, you can imagine that his life is completely different based on one choice. That kind of difference is what Jesus is referring to when he says a person is blessed when they are not offended. Living with offense creates a completely different life from living free of offense. Drinking the glass of offense is typically so subtle that people don't even know it's a choice they're making. They have no idea of the poison and how its potency will play out in the circumstances of their life. That's not the path you want. It doesn't produce the future you hope for.

Make your story the story of a blessed and unoffended life—a free life. It means there are no issues under the surface. It means there is no holding on to something that happened or something that was said. It means moving on, not just physically, but mentally, spiritually, and emotionally.

Study Questions

1. Can you relate to the five reasons not to be offended? Which one stands out the most to you?
2. Everyone gets served offense from time to time. But drinking the "poison of offense" is optional. How can people move forward and leave the offense behind?
3. Recall a time you've felt offended. Were you able to move on from that offense, or are you still carrying it with you today?
4. What do you need to do to become unoffendable?

CHAPTER 15

RELATIONSHIP OWNERSHIP

Adam and Eve were the first finger-pointing couple on the planet. When things went wrong, Adam said to God, "It's the woman's fault." Eve said, "It's the devil's fault." Ever since then humanity has become experts in making excuses, playing the victim, and shifting the blame. Owning our story means that we own our relationships fully and completely.

The first thing you might think when you hear that is, *C'mon, Kevin, a relationship is a two-way street. How can I be accountable for a relationship when the other person is being a complete jerk? They are unreasonable, irrational, and impossible to talk to.*

Owning your relationship doesn't mean you are responsible for what other people do. It means that you accept responsibility for everything you do and for everything you bring into the relationship:

- Your attitudes
- Your feelings and emotions
- Your perspective
- Your body language
- Your words
- Your investment

Rather than playing the victim, passing the blame or making excuses, you take full responsibility to be the best you that you can be.

By the way, if this sounds risky or daring, this is just a reminder that this is not a book about being guarded and playing it safe. It's about being open, being vulnerable, and risking exposure. Owning every part of our story means we make a move when there's no guarantee of the outcome.

If you want your relationships to be healthy and strong, one of the best things you can do is to have a full-ownership policy, where you take personal responsibility and ownership of your relationships. Scripture says that there's power in agreement and that "two are better than one" (Eccles. 4:9), meaning that the more people in a relationship do this, the stronger and healthier the relationship is. But if we're going to own our story, we can't wait for others to adopt an ownership mindset; we have to do it whether anyone else does or not. "Each of you must take responsibility for doing the creative best you can with your own life" (Gal. 6:5 MSG). This means taking full ownership of your life and relationships. Not 50 percent, not 80 percent, but 100 percent ownership. I'm not saying this is easy, because it's not.

In fact, most of us have been conditioned to place the responsibility for our lives on something or someone other than ourselves.

And so you have to have a policy to take on full ownership of your life. This is what the policy looks like:

THE FULL-OWNERSHIP POLICY =
All In, No Victim, No Blame, No Excuses

THE FULL-OWNERSHIP POLICY MEANS THAT YOU'RE ALL IN

A few years back we sat down with a financial advisor, and as we looked at our savings accounts, we were surprised that we hadn't managed to create greater returns in our IRA accounts. The financial advisor then shared that what was happening to us was common. He said that people tend to overestimate how much they've invested and feel disappointed when they see that the size of the return is not what they expected. He said, "You're getting back based on what you're putting in. If you want more out, you have to put more in." I think this is common not only in savings accounts but in every area of life. People tend to see themselves as putting more into life and relationships than they actually are. They overestimate the size of their investment into their work, their marriage, their kids, their friendships, their church as being much bigger than it is, and then they are disappointed and feel cheated when they don't see the returns they expected in those same areas of life.

It's as if they give themselves credit for a level 10 investment when they actually made a level 4 investment. Then, they get a level 4 return and feel cheated. Those unmet expectations are typically blamed on something else or someone else rather than realizing that what they thought was a level 10 investment was actually a moderate level 4 investment. You can't get a level 10 return on a level 4 investment.

For example, it's common for people to go to church, keep to themselves, arrive late, leave fast, stay uninvolved, and then tell their friends that the church wasn't a friendly place. In thirty-four years of pastoring, I've never seen anyone come to church and go all in who didn't have tons of people surrounding them, loving them, and eager to help them in every way possible. It just doesn't happen.

Going all in will always, without fail, create an all-in kind of harvest. This doesn't mean every idea works or every plan works. It means that wholehearted commitment always creates an outcome that far exceeds that of a partial, cautious, guarded approach. Scripture teaches us, "Whatever you do, work at it with all your heart, as working for the Lord" (Col. 3:23).

All in. Not holding back, not keeping score, not waiting to see what others will do. Not tentative, not calculated, not having an agenda. But instead, facing outward, being eager, being ready to serve, being helpful, speaking encouragement, extending hospitality, being always considerate, being kind, and being generous. Being vulnerable is being all in when there's no guarantee of the outcome.

Whether it's our relationship with God or with other people, relationships move forward at the speed of commitment and stay as they are without it. Just for the record, I told Sheila I loved her before she told me she loved me. I guess I was tired of her chasing me. I was hoping, however, that she would say she loved me, too. But it didn't happen. She's always been good at changing the subject on a dime, and she was in top form that night as she left me hanging there as the only one ready to say the L word. Obviously, she came around and realized she didn't want to miss out on the best thing that ever happened to her!

Joking aside, a strong, healthy marriage is always that of two people who are both all in. It's not a 50-50 partnership. Marriage is a 100-100 partnership. All it takes to mess up a marriage is for one person to stop giving 100 percent. If the husband is giving only 50 percent energy and effort, the wife can't do more than 100 percent. She can't do 150 percent. The relationship starts to suffer because one person is not all in.

Jesus' leadership philosophy differentiated between a hireling and a good shepherd (see John 10:1–5). One tells of somebody who likes having a position or job security. The other has an *all-in* commitment to shepherding and lays down his or her life in that commitment.

When we look for a team to put around us in ministry, we know that there's a huge difference between a hireling and a person who is all in, heart and soul. At times we've needed a skill that a hireling could bring us, and working with the hireling is completely different from working with the one who is committed to the cause. The hireling asks different questions, has different values, and compartmentalizes their commitment to fit into a formula and a schedule. Although they may provide a skill you need, they lack the heart to persevere in pressure and push forward into progress and growth. Hirelings are not evil. In fact, they can be helpful. You just don't want to confuse them with people who are all in, owners and stewards. People who are all in are dependable, reliable investors. They go above and beyond, and they do it with ease, with joy, with gratitude to get to do what they do.

THE FULL-OWNERSHIP POLICY MEANS THAT YOU WON'T PLAY THE VICTIM

The victim mentality is the attitude of people who see themselves as victims of circumstances as well as other people's choices and actions.

One of the things we do through the work of our Champions Foundation, a nonprofit created through our church, is to provide a home for orphaned children in South Africa. Many of the children we support are infected by the HIV virus. These children are not suffering the consequences of their choices, but the choices of others. They become infected with HIV during pregnancy, childbirth, or breastfeeding. There are 1.7 million AIDS orphans in South Africa alone and 16.5 million worldwide.

It was at our Champions Forever Home that we first met

Naomi and learned about her story. When she was ten years old, her stepfather threw hot scalding water on her and her mother. When she attempted to fight back, he threw kerosene on her and lit a match. She lay in the house for five hours before help arrived. She suffered tremendously, was not expected to live, and thought at times how to take her own life. Two years later, she was in a church service listening to a message on forgiveness when she felt God tell her it was time to let go of the deep hate and anger and forgive her stepdad. Since then she has had several surgeries to manage the scarring on her body. She is recovering physically, but even better, she is quick to talk about the power of forgiveness and share her big hopes and dreams for the future. Today she is working in a nonprofit organization helping orphans find forever families.

Owning your story means owning every part of it, even the part in your past that was out of your control, the part when someone else's actions and choices had a negative impact on your life. Maybe your parents divorced, and it created hardship for you. Maybe you grew up without one or both of your parents. You may have been bullied by someone in your school or neighborhood. You may have been blamed for something you didn't do. Owning your story means coming to terms with the idea that life isn't fair. Everyone has some measure of injustice in their story. The good news is that this reality doesn't leave us helpless and hopeless, because alongside the undeserved hardship are the undeserved blessings. Life is hard, but God is good!

The fact that life isn't fair is not only bad news; it's also good news. It means we are the beneficiaries of undeserved goodness and grace. The same way that Adam through disobedience opened the door of undeserved hardship, Jesus through obedience opened the door of undeserved favor and blessings in our life. Thankfully, because of God's abundant grace and goodness, we don't get what we deserve; we get what grace provides.

People who have a victim mentality don't know they have it, so do a checkup from the neck up by listening carefully to the words you say and the thoughts you think. Listen for any dead-end, conclusive conversation about your life and your circumstances. Do you refer to yourself as an overcomer or a victim of circumstances? Do you talk about what someone else said or did to explain why you can't get ahead or make progress in your life, your job, your ministry?

If so, that's a victim mentality. The victim is trapped and will stay trapped where they are until they trade in the victim mindset for a victory mindset. When you play the victim, you stay the victim, but when you own your story, you become a recipient of God's power to overcome. Whatever is born of God overcomes the world (see 1 John 5:4), which means that nothing and no one else has the power to hold us back from an overcoming life. The only one who can hold you back is you. Don't let that happen. Don't surrender the outcome of your story to negative events or circumstances in your life. Keep owning the outcome regardless of the circumstances. When you do that, your worst days become your best days. The problem becomes the possibility. The victim becomes a victor.

THE FULL-OWNERSHIP POLICY MEANS YOU WON'T
SHIFT THE BLAME

Blame shifting is projecting blame on other people for conditions in our own lives. We start blaming others at an early age, usually to escape getting into trouble but also to make ourselves look good. Then the behavior sticks, often well into our adult life. I'm sure you see people point fingers all the time. It's become common and acceptable for people to blame their boss, the government, the president, the church, their spouse, their parents, their coach, their teacher. Team members complain that their leader doesn't give them direction, meaning they can't get anything done unless they're told what to do. Leaders, on the other hand, complain about what they allow rather than changing it. Blaming people keeps us from owning our story.

- If everything is someone else's fault, then what part do we play in our own lives?
- Do our choices have consequences?
- If energy is spent on blaming, then what is left for owning?
- If we can make our problems someone else's fault, will we ever know the real reasons for the problems?

Owning your story is not about taking blame or placing blame. It's about owning the outcome. It's about embracing the place where you are and moving forward toward something better. If you've done something wrong and an apology is in order, then certainly give it, but understand that blaming yourself or others is a complete waste of time and energy.

THE FULL-OWNERSHIP POLICY MEANS YOU DON'T MAKE EXCUSES

Excuses are the reason or explanation people use to release themselves from relational responsibility. You can make progress or you can make excuses, but you can't do both.

Sheila and I bought property and built a house on land that had apple and cherry trees. The trees had not been pruned for years, so they looked worn down, and the fruit looked bad and had bugs in it. We could have come up with all kinds of excuses to leave them that way. We could have said we're not horticulturists and we don't know anything about fruit trees. We could have said someone else planted the trees. Not only that, we could have said it was the previous owners' fault that the trees were not doing well and just left them alone. We could have gone spiritual in our excuses and said that if God wanted the trees to do better, He could have done something with them.

> You can make progress or you can make excuses, but you can't do both.

But we were now owners. Those trees were now our trees. They were on our property, so we took responsibility for the health of those trees, and as we invested in the trees, they started getting weighed down with good fruit. We had apples and cherries in abundance.

Jesus said, "Make the tree good and the fruit will be good" (Matt. 12:33). He was saying that if you want good fruit in your life, your career, and your relationships, don't be an observer or a bystander; be an owner. Make the tree good and its fruit will be good.

You can see your relationships as something you are not responsible for, or you can see your relationships as trees of opportunity you are taking full responsibility for. It's the same with your finances, your health, your successes, and your failures. When the fruit is not healthy and good, you can play the victim, apply the blame, and make excuses, *or* you can adopt the full-ownership policy—you have an all-in, no victim, no blame, no excuses mindset.

Study Questions

1. What does "ownership in a relationship" mean to you after reading this chapter?
2. Discuss or reflect on the Full Ownership Policy: All In, No Victim, No Blame, No Excuses.
3. Think of a relationship in your own life. What area do you need to own rather than passing the blame?
4. Have you ever played the victim in a relationship? How can you overcome the victim mentality and change your thinking?

CHAPTER 16

RELATIONAL MATHEMATICS

Relationships never leave us where they find us; they always affect our lives in one way or another. Much like mathematics, relationships can take away strength and create deficiency, or they can add strength and create synergy.

God's plan for your life includes people. Lots of people. You're not meant to do life alone. But you're also not meant to do life with everyone. *Not everyone who is good to you is good for you.* If you're serious about owning your story and being all that you are meant to be, it's absolutely essential that you learn to differentiate the wrong people and surround yourself with the right people. This next section is to help you identify four kinds of people who have already come and are coming into your life.

> Not everyone who is good to you is good for you.

SUBTRACTORS

Subtractors take strength from you. There's a difference between you offering strength to someone and someone weakening you. The story of Samson and Delilah is a good example of this. He didn't realize it, but Delilah was taking his strength from him.

Having said that, in most cases, subtractors are not out to hurt you. Sometimes they are emotionally needy people. Other times, they can be people with negative attitudes who always see the glass as half-empty. In work-related environments they might have lids on their competence that hinder them from continuing to add value. These are just a few examples of subtractors. If you try to help them, make sure you do it from a place of strength and not from a feeling of guilt. If you're not gifted and knowledgeable in the area of their need, don't make the mistake of assuming you can turn the subtractors into adders. Love them, want the best for them, pray for them, but know your own limits and stay focused on your God-given purpose.

DIVIDERS

Dividers separate you from the right people. Sometimes it's intentional and divisive, but usually it's not as intentional as it is directional. They are headed in a different direction from where the right people are headed. The deeper your relationship is with these people (oftentimes your own family or close friends), the more difficult it can be to stay connected to the people God has connected you to.

I call the people God wants to connect you to God-assigned connections. They are the VIPs in your life. Sometimes they are up close relationally, and other times they are a voice that can mentor you from a distance. Either way, when God puts their voice in your life, it's up to you to recognize who they are and stay close and connected to them.

Don't let dividers get in between you and a God-assigned connection.

ADDERS

Adders encourage you and make you better. They contribute and add strength to your life. When you are with them or around them, you get bigger on the inside, more aligned with your values, and inspired to be the person you are meant to be. Honor these people. Express appreciation to them, listen to them, and learn from them.

A word of caution, though: When God brings people into your life to add to who you are, don't make the mistake of comparing yourself to them or competing with them. The minute you do, you eliminate what they are meant to bring into your life.

MULTIPLIERS

Multipliers provide resources to you and unite you with others for a common purpose. Your world gets bigger and better when they are in it. Don't assume that a multiplier is just a networker. Multipliers don't just do favors for people who want an introduction to someone they know. Multipliers are a level beyond that. They are people who believe in you and use their platform and relational equity to expand yours. They open doors of opportunity and connect you to people who have a common purpose, and the introduction will benefit you and the multiplier.

Make sure you recognize this as something God does and not something you expect. You don't pick them; God does. It's a God-ordained, organic, unforced blessing of God when a multiplier comes into your life. Honor them, express ongoing gratitude to them, and look for ways to bless them for what they bring into your life.

BE THE RIGHT PERSON

In the previous two chapters we talked about being healthy and unoffendable. I know this isn't an official word, but come along with me and smile as you consider this:

- Who you *be* has a lot to do with the *we*, and the *we* has a lot to do with who you *be*.
- It's best to put the *be* before the *we*. In other words,

decide who you are going to *be* versus letting the *we* define who you *be*.

- When who you *be* is right, then the right *we* is formed. With the wrong *we* you'll never become who you're really meant to *be*.

Are you smiling?

Part of what I do is to serve leaders, specifically pastors, helping them become the best they can be. Leaders come in all shapes and sizes, but more often than not leaders are type A personalities, who tend to be very competitive and self-critical, which often leads to them being loners and isolating themselves from people they could benefit from having in their life.

You would assume that type A personalities would love being together, but often that's not the case. Their tendency to base their value on what they do can create a need to be valued equally in every setting. When they are together, not everyone can lead, which means the ones who are not leading have no outlet for the grace that's on them to lead.

The good news is that I'm seeing more type A personalities who are successfully separating who they are from what they do. My observation is that the emerging type A leaders are more self-aware. They take better care of themselves, listen more, reflect more, ask more questions, and are more focused on *being* not just *doing*.

When this happens, it is a huge win for all of us, because these leaders are becoming a better version of themselves. It doesn't mean it's easy for them, but it does mean huge wins for everyone when leaders are focused on who they *be*. They form alignment and work together, and everyone benefits. They win, their family wins, their church or company wins, and most important, God wins. Again, this enormous win that benefits so many people is the result of leaders *being* the right person.

There are a few more things I need to tell you about relational mathematics and how it's different from basic arithmetic. You already know that relationships are not as simple as a math formula you learn in first grade and can count on the rest of your life. In fact, relational math will sometimes require you to go against what the math teacher taught you in school.

SOMETIMES YOU HAVE TO SUBTRACT TO ADD

In arithmetic, subtraction is the opposite of addition, but in relationships, before the right people can be added, the wrong people have to be subtracted. The wrong people always hinder the right people from coming and staying in your life.

You might be at a place in your life where you could use some positive input and encouragement that the people around you can't provide. In fact, if you look around at the people closest to you and all you see are people who talk about their problems or gossip about other people, you're trapped in smallness with the wrong people. You're surrounded by people who are going nowhere and complaining in the process. But that's not what God wants for you. He wants you to rise up out of that. He wants you to be confident and know in your heart that there's something better out there for you.

You can't expect Positive Paul to come hang out with your friend Negative Ned. Oil and water don't mix. But you can make a decision to not stay where you are surrounded by people who only pull you down or hold you back. Don't assume that God wants you to open your life to everyone. No, He wants you to:

- Be cautious in friendship (see Prov. 12:26).
- Avoid being friends with fools (see Prov. 13:20) and hot-tempered people (see Prov. 22:24).
- Do as much life as possible with people who sharpen you and make you better and wiser (see Prov. 27:17; 13:20).

The amazing thing is that when you relationally reposition yourself, free up the inner circle of your life, and start to be the person you long to be, the people you belong with will be drawn in to your life. They will come! Faith-filled people, encouraging people, people who live with hope and confidence will be added into your life.

TWO HALVES DON'T MAKE A WHOLE

It's pretty common for single people to say, "I'm looking for my other half." Sometimes it's just lighthearted semantics that express a desire to find the right person. Other times it's a perception that a person has about themselves that they are never going to be happy unless someone makes them happy. They assume that their mood swings will be gone. Their fluctuating attitude will be stable. Their battle with low self-esteem will not be an issue when someone has fallen in love them and is living life with them. But nothing could be further from the truth.

Yes, in arithmetic one half plus one half equals one whole. But in a relationship, one half plus one half equals two different one halves. If you're not whole going into marriage, you won't be whole because of marriage. If you don't overcome bad moods when you're single, marriage won't remedy you of moodiness. Based on how the two of you are coming together, these things are true:

- Two immature people coming together doesn't make for a mature relationship.
- Two insecure people coming together doesn't make for a secure relationship.
- Two unhealthy people coming together doesn't make for a healthy relationship.

But the opposite is true as well:

- Two mature people will have a mature relationship.
- Two secure people will have a secure relationship.
- Two healthy people will have a healthy relationship.

Whatever you are before you're married is what you bring into the marriage. The best thing you can offer another person is a healthy you, a whole you. That's not just true for people not yet married; it's true for all of us who are married. Being healthy, staying whole, being our best, taking care of ourselves physically, spiritually, and emotionally is the best gift we can give the people that we love. Because in marriage two whole people equals one amazingly healthy marriage.

TWO ARE BETTER THAN ONE

This is a reference to the synergy that togetherness creates. It applies to those who would assume that relationships are not worth the effort we put into them, that having a spouse and family is all they can handle, and outside of that, it's better to keep to themselves.

I know it's easy to feel that way when you've had relationships that were complicated. I get that, because I've had, and still have, a few of those myself. I've come to realize that as much as possible I want to do life with uncomplicated people. People who believe the best. People who don't read something into what you say, causing you to constantly watch how you say things and overexplain yourself. People who are stable and secure in themselves, open in conversation, not moody, not easily offended. These uncomplicated people are not perfect, but once you've had complicated relationships, you have a great appreciation for the uncomplicated ones.

When like-minded, uncomplicated relationships come

together, it's far better than being alone. Especially, when there's a common goal. There are three great reasons given in the verses below for why togetherness is better:

Two people are better off than one, for they can help each other succeed. [*Success*] If one person falls, the other can reach out and help. But someone who falls alone is in real trouble. [*Safety*] Likewise, two people lying close together can keep each other warm. But how can one be warm alone? A person standing alone can be attacked and defeated, but two can stand back-to-back and conquer. Three are even better, for a triple-braided cord is not easily broken. [*Strength*] (Ecclesiastes 4:9–12 NLT)

The writer is saying that in a healthy, life-giving relationship we help each other succeed, stay safe, and grow stronger. Who wouldn't want that? See, God never intended us to do life alone. We're all meant to do life with other people, specifically with God's people. We are formed for family. We are created for community. The only way you can be all you are meant to be is to be connected, committed, and in community with God's people. When you're in a healthy community with like-minded people, you can't help but get bigger on the inside.

That doesn't mean that those people are perfect, nor does it mean their struggles are any less than yours. It also doesn't mean that it's easy or without challenges. But it does mean we should never buy into the idea that we are better off keeping our distance from people. Owning your story means persevering to stay connected in community. If you're not part of a local church, you're missing out on God's plan for your life. Don't let other ideas, past experiences, or current fears hold you back. If you've withdrawn or been distant, just know that part of getting bigger on the inside means pushing past self-imposed limits to engage and be an active part of God's great family.

Study Questions

1. What does it mean in relational mathematics when we say, "sometimes you have to subtract to add"?
2. Think of some of the people that have been adders and multipliers in your life. In what ways have they added to or multiplied back into your life?
3. What are three reasons Scripture says two are better than one? (See Eccles. 4:9–12)

FIGHT FOR YOUR FUTURE

"You can't go back and change the beginning, but you can start where you are and change the ending."

—C. S. Lewis

"Our greatest weapon against stress is our ability to choose one thought over another."

—William James

"You may have to fight a battle more than once to win it."

—Margaret Thatcher

CHAPTER 17

BEING YOUR BEST
IN THE STRESS

Goliath, the Gittite, is the most well-known giant in history. He was over nine feet tall. He wore bronze armor that weighed about 125 pounds and a bronze helmet, and he carried a bronze javelin slung over his shoulder. A soldier walked in front of him, carrying his shield.

It was common in that day for two armies in conflict to choose one warrior to represent each side in a fight to the death. Goliath is described as a champion out of the camp of the Philistines. He came to the battle lines for forty days, calling for a warrior from the army of Israel to meet him in battle. The fight was not just a pride fight to see who would win. It was not a pay-per-view with money and titles as the prize. The outcome of this fight would determine the future of the nation of Israel. The Philistines wanted to capture the mountain ridge near Bethlehem and split Saul's kingdom in two. If they succeeded, the people of Israel would become their slaves. Even though that's not the future that anyone in the army of Israel wanted, when the call to battle was given, none of the soldiers stood up to fight. Not one. Nada.

David, still a teenager, was on the battlefield one day, delivering supplies to his older brothers. In desperation, King Saul had sweetened the pot by adding some personal rewards for anyone who would fight and kill Goliath. The message spread through the ranks: For the man who fights and wins, his father's house has tax-free status, and he will have the king's daughter's hand in marriage—which translated into fame and fortune.

In the noisy chaos, David didn't hear the announcement clearly, so he asked the soldiers around him to repeat it. He wanted to make sure he was hearing everything right. David was thinking about the future. I think it's fair to assume a conversation similar to this was going on in David's mind: *What happens if I don't fight? If I don't fight, God has no opportunity to give us the victory. If I don't fight, my nation is humiliated and will be slaves to our enemies. If I don't fight, there's no hope for the future. On the other hand, if I fight, God will give us the victory. If I fight, my nation will be free of this oppression. If I fight, there's a bright future ahead for me and my family.*

This is where it all started for David. It was his first window versus street moment that would actually be seen by thousands of people. The king and the entire army sat in the window that day while David headed toward the streets. You could say it was his first big dance. It was a decision he would make over and over again in his life. Nobody forced him to fight, and nobody would have blamed him if he had turned away and gone home. Others would have agreed if he said he was unqualified or lacked the skills needed to face the giant.

Armed with nothing more than a sling and five stones, David decided to risk exposure and put himself out there when the odds were stacked against him. He entered the battle as 100–0 underdog. Most would say he had no chance. But David had checked all the boxes required to be used by God in a mighty way. He was prepared and ready for this moment and the instant fame that would follow.

The slinger of stones was at the top of his game and had negotiated for this opportunity. Goliath, the giant, was big on the outside, but David was bigger on the inside! The giant fell, and David cut off his head and delivered it as a trophy to his leader, King Saul.

The fight for your future is not a physical fight with an armor-clad giant on a hillside in Judea, but that doesn't mean it's less stressful or demanding.

THERE'S NO SUCH THING AS A STRESS-FREE LIFE

When the topic of stress comes up, it is usually to remind us of how stress can be harmful to our health and overall well-being. You rarely, if ever, hear that stress is part of a meaningful life.

As a young pastor attending leadership events, I would often hear warnings about stress and ways to avoid it. Sometimes it was even presented in ways that caused me to feel ashamed that I was working hard and putting in long hours in the trenches of "pastor-preneuring" our church. I never remember anyone explaining that stress actually has an upside. Not all stress is bad stress, and to live with no stress is an unreasonable goal if you want to have a meaningful life. There's no shame in stepping into stress. It doesn't mean you are doing something wrong, and it doesn't make you less spiritual.

Jesus had stress. In fact, Scripture says he sweated blood, which can happen when our body is reacting to extreme stress.

The disciples had stress. The mission they were on required them to embrace stress.

The heroes of the Bible had stress. Their goal was not to have a stress-free life.

Marriage has stress. When two different people (often opposite in personality) decide to do life together, they are committing themselves to a journey that includes its share of stress.

Family has stress. Children are a blessing, but parenting is stress on steroids.

You and I are no different. We will have stress if we have a job, and stress if we don't have a job. We'll have stress if we have lots of money or don't have any money. There's no such thing as a stress-free life!

In the movie *The Lion King*, Timon and Pumbaa (the meerkat and the warthog) try to convince Simba, a young lion cub, to go after the stress-free life. They called it *hakuna matata*, which translates from Swahili as "there are no troubles." It sounded great to young Simba, but the problem was that in the pursuit of *hakuna matata*, he would miss out on his future. Simba's father, Mufasa, was king of the Pride Lands, and Simba's destiny was to take over as the king. In the end he made the choice to give up the pursuit of a trouble-free life and embrace the problems and the stress that go along with a life of meaning and purpose.

What's true in Simba's story is true in our story. We have absolutely zero chance of living a stress-free life and a meaningful life at the same time.

GOD IS IN THE STRESS

Jesus taught us that there's no such thing as a *hakuna matata* life here on earth: "I have told you these things, so that in me you may have peace. In this world you will have trouble. But take heart! I have overcome the world" (John 16:33). Jesus is saying, "Trouble is unavoidable in the place that I have assigned to you. I've told you these things to give you peace in the trouble-filled, tension-filled places that I've assigned you to be." He's saying, "*My* peace, the peace that I can offer, is not limited to peaceful environments and peaceful circumstances. My peace goes with you into the places I'm sending you."

It always amazes me when I come across people who avoid pressure, because they want to be where God is, and they assume God's not in the stress. They think God stays in a quiet, calm setting with serene surroundings. That's like saying God keeps to the quiet outdoors and spas. Don't get me wrong; it's a good idea to go somewhere quiet and peaceful to get recharged. At the same time, we have to get free of the idea that God is only in the quiet places. We need to start seeing him in the noisy, loud, turbulent, pressure-filled places that he's assigned us to.

The good stuff happens in the place of pressure. Pressure is where giants fall. Pressure is where battles are won. Pressure is where diamonds are formed and babies are born.

The presence of problems doesn't mean the absence of God. While it's true that sometimes God wants us to leave the tension and go to the peaceful place, He's actually assigned us and called us to live in the wild. To stay in the streets. To have peace in the place of our assignment. God doesn't wait for us to leave the pressure cooker and come to Him in the quiet place. God is in the chaotic and tension-filled places, too. He is in the stress, too!

> The presence of problems doesn't mean the absence of God.

A close friend of our family's has been on a career path for several years, going after her dream to be a sports reporter. She's now working in the industry but continuing to pursue the opportunities in front of her. Recently she shared that on this journey she has felt anxious, stressed, overwhelmed, exhausted, and lonely. She's juggling six jobs at a time, commuting across the city, pushing herself to stay fit, and continuing her volunteer time at church. She told us recently how God has been with her, strengthening her and encouraging her in the toughest times and in the most difficult seasons on her path of purpose.

Everything that's worth something has a price. All progress has opposition and all advancement has adversity. When you find yourself in wild and crazy situations at school, at work, and in your family, you may feel tempted to withdraw or even run the other way. But before you do, ask yourself, *Is this where I'm meant to be? Is this what I'm here to do?* Because the place you want to run from is often the place God has assigned you to. If He assigned you to that place, He is with you in that place. Start to see Him there.

God was in Babylon with Daniel and closed the mouths of the lions. God was in Macedonia with Paul and Silas and opened the doors of their jail cell. God puts us in places that are stressful to achieve the work He wants to do in that place. But He doesn't just send us. He is there with us. God is in the stress.

STRESS IS NOT THE ENEMY

If you listed what means the most to you and what gives you joy, it would probably be things like your marriage, your ministry, your relationships, your family, your job, the cause you volunteer for, and the church community you belong to. The unique part of all of these is that they all have a level of stress that comes along with them. *The enemy is not the stress itself. The enemy is the smallness people feel in times of stress. It's the thoughts and attitudes they have when they experience stressful situations in their lives.*

If you see stress as the enemy, you'll focus on getting away from the stress rather than adjusting your thoughts so that you are bigger and stronger in the stress. Scripture says, David *ran toward* Goliath. Not away from him, but *toward* him. He was anxious in a different way from everyone else. Others were anxious to run away from the fight while David was anxious to run toward the fight. When everyone else saw the giant as a stress to avoid, David saw the giant as an opportunity too great to be ignored.

In the same way as David, people who are best in stress think differently in stress, which causes them to respond differently when they experience stress. These people process stress differently and end up with a better outcome. When you talk to a fitness trainer or a bodybuilder, you'll soon see that they think differently about going to the gym and lifting weights from the average person. The bodybuilder approaches the gym with vision, while others see it as an enemy that creates pain in their life.

Recently I talked to a bodybuilder who reiterated the process of strength training and muscle growth. He said that muscles are overloaded in weight training, causing muscles to tear from the stress, and then the muscle grows in the resting period. The process for getting stronger is to consistently put your body under stress followed by short intervals of rest.

Just like picking up weights will make us stronger physically, embracing stressful challenges with intervals for renewing our minds, resting, and worshipping will make us stronger mentally and spiritually. If your goal is to live your best and strongest life, don't think of stress as an enemy to avoid, but an opportunity to embrace.

CONVERTING STRESS INTO ENERGY THAT GOD CAN USE

On January 5, 2015, Bill Gates drank a glass of water that had been human waste five minutes earlier. It's a project he's been investing in that converts human feces into clean drinking water.[1] When I first heard about this, it sounded so ridiculous and irrational to me that something so contaminated could be converted into what can save and sustain life. But it's exactly what the project is designed to do. The hope is that everyone in the world could have access to clean drinking water because of a converter called an Omni Processor. These converters can be placed in villages and towns where there is no clean water supply. With more than 2.5 billion people lacking safe sanitation, a problem that kills seven hundred thousand children a year, the outcome would be to save a huge number of lives through safe water supplies.

Just like the Omni Processor, people who perform the most helpful human services are people who have learned to convert stress into useful energy. These are law enforcement officers, doctors and nurses in hospital emergency rooms, and pilots who keep us safe as we fly through heavy winds.

There's no doubt that when we embrace stress the right way, stressful situations can be converted into positive experiences. There is stress that goes along with education, business opportunities, personal growth, and financial growth. The greatest victories in all of these areas are reserved for people who process stress in a way that converts it into usable, helpful energy.

When you experience a challenge or pressure on your path of purpose, rather than thinking about how you can eliminate stress, consider how you can convert stress into energy that God can use. If you were to talk to any great athlete who has been strong in stress, they will tell you that the key to their success is not being free of stress but rather learning how to convert stress into a positive, useful, motivating energy that helps them win.

- The golfer standing over a putt, knowing that if he makes it, he will accomplish the dream he has worked for all his life.
- The basketball player at the free throw line with one second left and a chance to win the championship title.
- The field goal kicker who has a chance to win the Super Bowl with millions of people watching.

The pressure of those moments is inevitable. It's unavoidable. The greatest athletes are the ones who have run toward the stress and dreamed of being in that weighty, tension-filled moment where they have a chance to make history. The ones who rise up in those high-stress situations are the ones who have trained themselves to convert stress into a useful form. Those kinds of champions don't crumble under stress; they convert stress.

As believers, God has given us everything we need to overcome in even the most severe and stressful circumstances. It begins when we stop seeing stress as something to avoid and convert it into energy that God can use.

The writings of Isaiah provide one of the clearest descriptions in Scripture about stress conversion: "You will keep in perfect peace those whose mind is steadfast, because they trust in you" (Isa. 26:3).

You will keep in perfect peace. The word *perfect* is not in the Hebrew text. The original text reads, "peace peace," which is said twice to emphasize the extreme peace, the unconditional peace, enjoyment of peace, and the continuance of peace. *Peace Peace!*

Those whose mind is steadfast. This is the qualifying statement of guaranteed peace in your life. Perfect peace is for those whose thoughts are fixed and focused on the positive, affirming, reassuring promises of God.

Because they trust in you. They are steadfast and confident because they trust fully in the character and goodness of God regardless of the circumstances of life. God's peace comes to us from knowing that when life is hard, God is good.

Converting stress into a usable form is more about mind management than time management. If you put too much hope in a perfectly organized life, you will be stressed trying to keep it organized. Some of the most organized people are the most stressed people, because when they have their life completely organized, they are constantly stressing out to keep it that way. This is why mind management is more helpful in stress than time management. Some people try to beat stress by going to bed early, but going to bed early does no good if you can't sleep. If you want to be your best in the stress, the greatest key by far is the Isaiah approach to mind management. A steadfast, focused, fully trusting mindset converts stress into energy that God can use.

Study Questions

1. Consider that not all stress is bad stress. What are some examples of good stress that leads to positive outcomes?
2. Think of a time you've felt stressed in the past. Looking back, do you realize now that God was there to meet you in the midst of that situation? How did that situation push you to become stronger?
3. How can you begin to trust God's perfect peace in the midst of a stressful situation?
4. Discuss or reflect on: "The presence of problems doesn't mean the absence of God."
5. How can you capitalize on mind management to convert stress into usable energy?

CHAPTER 18

GIANT INTERRUPTIONS

When David left home that morning, Goliath wasn't in his plans. David was bringing food supplies to his brothers, who were serving in the army. David was doing what he was there to do, but suddenly the routine was interrupted by the sound of a commanding, angry voice in the distance that echoed through the valley. Everyone stopped what they were doing, and all attention was turned to the valley below, where Goliath had come to the battle line to make sure everyone knew that he wasn't going away.

David had never seen or heard of Goliath. He wasn't on David's radar, but you can tell David's first impression wasn't a good one. He asked, "Who is this uncircumcised Philistine?" (1 Sam. 17:26). In other words, "How did he get here? Where did he come from, and who does he think he is?"

I'm sure you can relate to the unwanted, uninvited,

unplanned giant interruption that busts down the door and steps into your world like a hostile takeover:

- The relationship you thought would last forever suddenly ends.
- The company you work for is downsizing, and you find yourself without a job.
- The person you trust breaks your heart.
- The baby you were excited to bring into the world doesn't make it to full term.

One of the greatest enemies of our future comes in the form of unplanned, unwanted interruptions. An unplanned and unwanted interruption is like a fight that starts with being sucker punched. The first punch catches us completely off guard, puts us in a daze, and creates an uncertainty about what to do next. Confusion and doubts come to the surface. The volume goes up on the voice of fear in our minds.

We experienced that when Jodi, our daughter, was in college, and doctors found and removed melanoma from her back. At that point, she was living her dream as a college athlete playing basketball on a full-ride scholarship. Her dad and mom were loving every minute of it (especially the scholarship). Then, one day as we stood in the kitchen, her phone rang. Jodi answered, and I watched her face the next few moments as she listened without saying a word. I could tell it wasn't good news. Then suddenly the conversation ended. As she hung up the phone, she managed to say, "The doctor doesn't feel like they got it all."

My first feeling was anger, almost outrage, at the doctor's office. *How can you just call my daughter and interrupt our life like this? She has plans, and this is not a part of it! She has places to go, people to see, and things to do.*

Prior to the call we knew that they had found melanoma. That was the first bad news. But when the nurse said that it had gone beyond what they had hoped, it definitely got real. That's what an unwanted interruption looks like. It rocks your world and throws you into an unexpected space between what has been and what will be.

Thankfully, the doctors were able to get all of the melanoma, and Jodi was able to get back to her life of school and basketball.

The truth is that we all have giant interruptions that force their way into our story. They call us to the battle lines again and again. The demand they place on us pulls us into a fight for our future. This is when we have to remember our part in our story. We are not just bystanders; we are influencers who have the final say in the story of our life.

AN INTERRUPTION IS AN OPPORTUNITY

Every interruption is an opportunity for us to press through our fear, push past our pain, and fight for God's will in our future. No matter what happens to us, we have the final say. We cast the final vote. We don't have to be victims of the unexpected interruptions. Every interruption is another opportunity to take our place in a long line of warriors who overcome in every battle they face: "No, in all these things we are more than conquerors through him who loved us. For I am convinced that neither death nor life, neither angels nor demons, neither the present nor the future, nor any powers, neither height nor depth, nor anything else in all creation, will be able to separate us from the love of God that is in Christ Jesus our Lord" (Rom. 8:37–39).

Being sons and daughters of God doesn't mean you can stop a crisis from happening, but it does mean you can conquer it. That's the essence of the ongoing fight for your future. You don't ignore the interruption and hope it goes away. You don't shrink back from it and lose your way. You face it with faith and fight your way through it.

GETTING THROUGH WHAT YOU'RE GOING THROUGH

1. Stay in the present.

Your first fighting stance when you're going through something is staying in the present. When your world is rocked by an unexpected interruption, negativity asserts itself by pulling you into regrets about the past or worries about the future. The truth is that you can't change the past, and what you do in the present is the only influence you have on the future. This means that when we're going through something, the best thing we can do is to "do today." Not replay yesterday, not speculate about tomorrow, but do something positive, beneficial, and helpful for today. Do something to move your life forward today. Put on some praise and worship music. Listen to an encouraging podcast. Get outdoors and get some exercise. Volunteer at church or in the community. Hang out with some positive people in a healthy atmosphere.

When you stay in the present mentally and emotionally, you protect yourself from regrets about the past or speculations about the future. Staying in the present is a fighting position that allows you to recover from the unexpected interruptions and position yourself to turn a setback into a comeback.

- Paul said, "Forgetting what is behind" (Phil. 3:13).
- Jesus said, "Do not worry about tomorrow…each day has enough trouble of its own" (Matt. 6:34).

When Jesus said, "do not worry about tomorrow," he was talking about catastrophizing. Catastrophizing is when you imagine how the current situation is making a catastrophe out of a future situation. When you imagine the worst, you then move quickly to catastrophic predicting, where you create the worst possible scenario in your mind about the future: Your best friend betrays you and you imagine that there's no way you can be happy without their friendship. You are let go from your position at work, and you imagine not being able to find another job and losing everything you have.

> ## Position yourself to turn a setback into a comeback.

When you do this, you experience high levels of anxiety and undermine the actual power you have in the present to influence the future. The truth is that you're never powerless. There's always something you can do. There's always a move you can make in the right direction.

The psalmist says, "This *is* the day that the LORD has made; We will rejoice and be glad in it" (Ps. 118:24 NKJV). Once you settle into a positive place in the present, you can begin to think about your future with faith and confidence. Until then, fight to stay in today. Fight to see the good in today. Fight to enjoy what you have today. Fight to have an attitude of gratitude today.

2. Lean into God's promises.

The second fighting stance when you're going through something is leaning into God's promises.

Our lives move in the direction of our words. Words are not just a sound we make; they are a creative force. Our words initiate life, strength or weakness, defeat or victory. God has promised us that when we're going through valleys, He is the God of the valleys. Storms of life will come, but He has promised to be with us in the storm. He promises us that when we believe and trust in Him, He is working all things together for our good.

The psalmist said his tongue is like the pen of a writer (see Ps. 45:1). James describes the tongue like a rudder on a boat (see James 3:4). When you put these two images from Scripture together you come up with a visual of what I call scripting and steering your life with your words. This is where you use your words to write the script of your future and then, moment by moment, day by day, steer yourself toward that future. Every time you open your mouth, you are scripting and steering. Every comment, every conversation, you're scripting and steering. Every morning when you get up, you're scripting and steering. This is what people of faith do. They use their words to steer their way through uncertainty and write the script for their future:

- Joshua said in times of uncertainty, "As for me and my household, we will serve the LORD" (Josh. 24:15).
- Paul, in reference to the battles he was fighting, said, "We are hard pressed on every side, but not crushed; perplexed, but not in despair; persecuted, but not abandoned; struck down, but not destroyed" (2 Cor. 4:8–9).

In another setting, Paul starts by saying what God has said, and then gives that as the reason for him saying what he says, "God has said, 'Never will I leave you; never will I forsake you.' So we say with confidence, 'The Lord is my helper; I will not be afraid'" (Heb. 13:5–6). This is what it looks like to lean into the promises of God: God said, so we say.

Words spoken are a creative force. Your words agree with

or contradict God's promises in your life. God wants to help you, lift you up, encourage you, empower you. Your enemy wants to hurt you, discourage you, destroy you. The words you choose will cast the final vote. Your words will align with the enemy's plans to steal, kill, and destroy, or your words will align with God's promise to give you a hope and a future.

When one of my grandsons was learning how to talk, he would sometimes grunt or point toward what he wanted. Rather than responding to his gestures, his mom would tell him, "Use your words." She wanted him to speak up and say what he wanted instead of continuing his lazy baby habits of pointing and grunting. God does the same with us. He waits for us to come into alignment with His promises. He waits for us to use our words to set the course of our future—to script and steer toward His promises in our lives.

3. Believe the possibilities.

The third fighting stance when you're going through something is believing the possibilities. When you live the life of an overcomer, today's tragedy is tomorrow's triumph. Our part is to engage in acts of faith even when we don't feel faith.

Rather than turn inward and become an observer or a window-watcher in your own life, choose to live outward with confidence demonstrated by integrating with the world around you. Rather than letting discouragement or fear hold you in the window, step out in the street, where you can mingle and engage with others. It will be encouraging to others and healing for us when we serve God's purpose in the place of our own pain.

When Don's wife passed away, Don was lonely and depressed. A neighbor invited him to Champions Centre, and his life and our church have not been the same since. He soon became a greeter, welcoming people with his big smile and generous gestures. When he was admitted to the hospital with pneumonia, Don said that he had so many visitors from the church that he thought they were going to have to bring bleachers into the room!

Why did so many people visit him in the hospital? Because Don left his lonely space—his place in the window—and started greeting and welcoming people at the door. What if Don had allowed himself to think that his life was over when his wife passed away? His story would have been very different if he had turned inward, felt sorry for himself, and allowed himself to think there's nothing he could do that mattered.

Most people assume when there is uncertainty that they have to turn inward for answers, so they pull back from life, relationships, serving, and going to church. No doubt, it can be helpful in the middle of an unexpected crisis to find more time alone and time with God one-on-one. The key is to do that while keeping a rhythm of *outward* living. It takes a belief in the possibilities to put ourselves in a place of openness toward people who can give counsel and advice and guide us toward health and healing. It also requires belief to know the help we need is not only in quiet places but also in the noisy interactive places of our life. Going inward causes us to want to spend time only with people who understand the space we're in. But the help and hope we need is not limited to people who understand. Some of what you need after a giant interruption is found only by serving and socializing with people, some of whom may not even know the space you're in.

You may remember in the first section of the book we said that vulnerability looks different in different settings and circumstances, but *vulnerability always requires courage.* Being vulnerable after a giant interruption means having the courage to engage with others in atmospheres that provide a life source you need. Things like love, joy, peace, wisdom, faith, and encouragement will spill on you when you put yourself in the right places with the right people.

In science, we see a picture of this synergy when a single molecule is vulnerable in pairing up with other molecules to create something better. For example, when hydrogen and oxygen come together to make water. Something better is created that neither molecule is capable of on its own. When we are joined with other people, the sum is greater than its parts. The outcome is better than what we can produce on our own.

Study Questions

1. Finish this statement: An interruption is an _____ _____.
2. Name three things you can do to "get through what you're going through."
3. What are some of God's promises that you can apply to your life today?

CHAPTER 19

GRAPES, GIANTS, AND GRASSHOPPERS

The people of Israel had been slaves in Egypt for four hundred years when God sent Moses with a message that he had future plans for them. Something better than the slavery. Something better than the poverty. The place God had for them was a place of promise and possibility where they could pioneer, be landowners, build houses, and create a legacy for their children's children. What followed is known in history as the Great Exodus, in which over 3 million slaves left Egypt on a journey to the land of promise.

When they finally arrived at the border, Moses sent spies in to explore the land. After they had been gone for forty days, they returned with a vine that had huge clusters of grapes, representing the richness of the land. They gave Moses a report that went something like this: "First, the good news: We brought back some incredibly large grapes to show you the fruitfulness of the land. The possibilities of this land are huge! Second, the not-so-good news: The people who live there are powerful. Their cities are large and walled, and there are also giants in the land."

THE GRAPES ARE REACHABLE

I want to assure you that God has grapes and more grapes planned for your future! He has "plans to prosper you and not to harm you, plans to give you a hope and a future" (Jer. 29:11). He has grapes with your name on them.

- Things you don't know about are in the works right now.
- He has opportunities He is bringing your way.
- He has doors that He is opening for you.
- He has good things scheduled in the days ahead.
- He has relationships and people He wants you to meet.
- He has prosperity planned for you and blessings that belong to you.

When the spies returned with grapes the size of watermelons, it was like each family had gone from slavery to winning the lottery. The grapes represented a future where the people who had a history of slavery would now own their own land, harvest their own crops, and never be poor again. They barely had time to get excited about their hopes and dreams because the spies announced that there were giants in the land of the grapes, which made it impossible for them to go there without dying or becoming slaves again.

The conversation went downhill from there. Imagine, here they are on the border of something better, and they're being told that the grapes are unreachable. This same scenario is the reality of everyone who hopes for a better future. God has grapes planned for us, but the land of the grapes is also the land of the giants. This is where you have a decision to make. Do you play it safe and stay where you are, or do you put yourself out there, risk exposure, abandon smallness, and fight for your future? Do you stay in the window, where you feel safe, or do you leave your comfort zone, head for the streets, embrace the stress, and fight for your future?

> God has grapes planned for us, but the land of the grapes is also the land of the giants.

One of the mistakes people make is to assume: *If God wants me to have something, I don't have to do anything; he will just cause it to happen in my life. I won't have to work for it. There shouldn't be any stress or pressure in the process.* They assume that if God wants them to have something, it will drop in their lap. If it doesn't happen, that means God must not have wanted it to happen. That thought has caused a lot of people to be passive and miss out on the possibilities, the blessings, the opportunities, the progress, and the legacy that God has planned for them.

The truth is that you will always face resistance between where you are and all that God has for you in your future. There are giants you will have to face and battles you will have to win. Yes, God is with you and for you, but you will have to fight for the future God has for you and your family.

Ronnie serves as an usher at Champions Centre. He wrote an email a while back sharing a bit of his journey and thanked his team leader for the privilege of being on the usher team. He said that growing up, he didn't really like people outside of his family and small circle of friends. People "annoyed" him, and so he had no problem emotionally hurting or distressing others. He said that it was common for him to get into conflicts, confrontations, and even fights with people. He went on to say:

One day a little over four years ago, I was sitting in what I call my "in and out seat" at Champions Centre, because since 2007 I would sit in the same seat, listen to the message, not talk to anyone, and just leave. That was my norm until one day I noticed no one was in "Chuck's" tunnel. [Chuck was an usher who had served for years and, since this note, unexpectedly went to heaven.] It seemed like the usher team was short on people that day, so I got up, walked down there, and started seating people. An usher thanked me, and even sent me an email again thanking me, and invited me back the next week. So next week I showed up to a morning huddle. I was incredibly nervous because, remember, I hated people.

He summed it up by saying:

The team at Champions Centre has invited me to be a part of something bigger than myself and how to love on people outside of my comfort zone. I've not only changed how I see people on a weekend but during the week as well. I found that showing love in conversation or a simple smile can make a person go from being angry and impatient to joyful and happy. It's now my personal goal just to make people smile. Serving on this team has changed my life and taught me to love people like Jesus did.

Ronnie sat for years in isolation at our church. He was meeting no one, serving no one, and unaware that he was creating a future of self-imposed boundaries and limitations. Thankfully, he didn't stay there. Thankfully, he left his "in and out seat," which he could still be sitting in today. He took steps of courage, and now he's walking in a future that he would have never had if he had stayed where his fears told him to stay. Today, he's not only experiencing a better life; he's experiencing a better relationship with Jesus. He's creating a different future than he would have had and encouraging others in the process. This is what happens when we press through our hesitations, fight through our reservations, and put ourselves out there. It feels risky and uncomfortable anytime we do this, but it's these kinds of moves that put us in the land of the grapes.

Lots of people sit in our churches with "do not disturb" signs on their faces. They hesitate when it's time to step up. They hold back when it's time to help out. Don't be that person. Be brave enough to be vulnerable, to step out, to drop your guard and take some risks. The best things happen when people make moves when there's no guarantee of the outcome.

If you're Simon Peter, making a move means stepping out of the boat in the middle of a windstorm. Yes, after a few steps, Peter sank, but Jesus was right there to put his hand out and pull him up. To this day, he's the only human to walk on water.

If you're Paul and Silas, making a move means having the courage to worship at midnight, when you have suffered and been put in jail for being a Christ follower. That move on their part opened the doors of that prison and led them to freedom: "The righteous shall move onward and forward; those with pure hearts shall become stronger and stronger" (Job 17:9 TLB). What does moving onward and forward look like for you? What's your next move?

- Is your next move to have a conversation that you keep putting off?
- Is your next move to start serving, stewarding, giving, helping?
- Is your next move to continue to do what you're doing now but doing it with all your heart? Being fully invested and all in?

In our church, there are three promises we've made as leaders and team members. One of the promises is to keep advancing. We have made that promise to ourselves, to one another, and to the unreached people of our city. We will not stay where we are or as we are, because to do so would be against the nature of our God, who so loved the world and who cared enough for each of us that he saved us and brought us into his family. To keep advancing means we believe that grapes and more grapes are in front of us—and are reachable.

THE GIANTS ARE DEFEATABLE

There is probably no verse that I've quoted over the years more often than "No weapon formed against you will prosper" (Isa. 54:17 NKJV). There's something about that promise and the ones following it that never get old to me and never fail to bring confidence to my soul.

The giants that you and I face are not physical giants but resistance in various forms that will hold us back and hinder us from moving forward. The giants we face come in many different forms, shapes, and sizes. As I'm writing this book, I'm dealing with distractions, brain blocks, and motivation dips as I move forward to finish what I started. The most challenging space is always the space between where you are now and where you're meant to be in the future. That's because there is always resistance on the path of purpose.

Mark was twenty-two years old when he landed in Los Angeles in 1982. He had no job, no place to live, and only a few hundred bucks to his name. He had served in the British military but had never gone to college. Within a few days he interviewed and was able to land a job as a nanny for a wealthy Beverly Hills family. Despite having no experience as a nanny, Mark went on the interview. The couple, realizing the advantage of having a nanny and security at the same time, hired him. While he was a nanny for two years, he was also putting together his first business plan, which was to buy T-shirts at $2 and sell them at $15–18. He didn't have a shop. He rented ten feet of space along a fence on a busy sidewalk at Venice Beach. Today, Mark Burnett is one of the top television producers in the world. He is the executive producer of six network television shows, including *Shark Tank* (ABC), *Survivor* (CBS), and *The Voice* (NBC). Burnett and his wife, Roma Downey, are strong Christians and have used their success to produce popular faith-based series—*The Bible* and *A.D. The Bible Continues*—as well as the feature films *Son of God, Little Boy, Woodlawn,* and *Ben-Hur*.[1]

Burnett's story is an example of someone who had no money, no home, and small beginnings but got bigger and stayed big on the inside. Imagine, a British soldier starting off as a nanny and then a street vendor T-shirt salesman who stayed confident in the pursuit of his dream. The pursuit of any calling, any mission, any venture will solicit resistance: Nothing of value comes easy. Whether it's writing a book or a song, building a business, losing weight, getting your degree, raising your kids, or leaving a lasting legacy, the space between where you are now and the goal you have for your future is filled with opposition. It's not personal; it's universal. It's not just you who is experiencing the challenge in moving forward. Everyone who has a vision for their life and a desire to move life forward will face challenges. Know this: There's always giant opposition in the space between where you are and where you are meant to go in the future, which is why the majority of the people around you will never reach their promised land. They give up rather than fight for it.

Joshua and Caleb were the only ones in the group of spies who came back with a confident report for Moses. While everyone else said they couldn't go forward, these two men said the opposite. They said, "We can certainly do it." "Caleb silenced the people before Moses and said, 'We should go up and take possession of the land, for we can certainly do it'" (Num. 13:30). I love the fact that Caleb used the word *certainly*. He didn't say, "Let's give it a try. We might have what it takes to win this fight." No, the faith in him was bigger than the giants in front of him. Even though others never made it, Caleb ended up with a home address in Canaan because he had a "certainly we can do it" attitude.

YOU'RE NO GRASSHOPPER

There was a heated debate that broke out that day at Kadesh in the desert of Paran. The majority of spies were overwhelmed by feelings of smallness. It was clear that the biggest issue in the debate was not about the amazing potential of the land. Nor was it the fact that there were giants in the land. The argument was about self-concept: how they saw themselves. For those who were opposed to moving forward toward the land of promise, their main issue was internal smallness. Here's what they said: "We seemed like grasshoppers in our own eyes, and we looked the same to them" (Num. 13:33).

They chose the smallest and ugliest of desert creatures they could think of to describe how they saw themselves compared to the giants. The fight for your future is more internal than external. Your greatest enemy is not the giants in your life. Your greatest enemy is how you see yourself compared to the giants in your life. The grasshopper mentality is a distorted view that will cause you to underestimate yourself, exclude yourself, doubt yourself, and ultimately disqualify yourself from the future God offers you. The greatest enemy of your future is not what happens to you; it's how you see yourself when it happens. The greatest enemy is not the loss of a relative, the loss of a job, or a financial setback. It's not a relationship that went bad or a personal failure. It's not your critics. It's how you see yourself after the loss or the setback. It's how you see yourself after you hear the criticism, read the email, or make a mistake. When you see yourself small, you count yourself out of the future God has for you.

> The greatest enemy of your future is not what happens to you; it's how you see yourself when it happens.

Your self-concept is based on your own evaluation of yourself. It's what you believe about you. Self-concept is something you may attempt to hide and keep close to you until you're in a place where situational demands are placed on you. In that moment or that setting, the manner with which you engage other people reveals a lot about your self-concept. It also affects how others view you. When the spies were giving their report to Moses they said, "We seemed like grasshoppers in our own eyes, and we looked the same to them." In other words, their own self-concept was also the way others saw them.

If you're hoping others will see your potential, your strengths, and your ability, you have to first see your potential, your strengths, and your ability. When you're not sure who you are, others won't be sure, either. But when you know who you are and what you're capable of, it causes you to present yourself in a way that others can see your strength.

A pastor friend of mine who knows I am a baseball Cardinals fan is friends with the former player and manager Joe Girardi. He sent me a bat signed by Joe. But it wasn't just signed by Joe. It reads, "To Kevin, best wishes, Joe Girardi." But here's the funny twist to the story: Joe signed this to another Kevin. It was sitting in his garage, and my friend said, "I know a Kevin who would love to have that bat!" I got the bat, put it in my office, and act like I'm the Kevin on the bat, but I know I'm not the Kevin on the bat. I wanted to be, but I'm not. I did what any sports fan would do. I kept it to myself and decided to go with it, acting like I'm the Kevin that Joe signed the bat to. The story doesn't stop there. Because later, when I was on a book tour, I got to talk to Joe Girardi. I told him the funny story about the bat, which means I'm now officially the Kevin who he gave the bat to.

We're all called to believe that what God says about us is true even when it doesn't feel like it applies to us. Scripture says, "Let the weak say I am strong." It doesn't say, "Let the weak admit their weakness." No, it's telling us to believe and declare that we're strong even though we've felt weak, been weak, looked weak, acted weak. The point is, you will never become strong by declaring how weak you are. The only way you get stronger is to start saying,

I'm strong.
I'm stronger than I think I am.
I am made in the image of God.
I am loved by God.
I am a conqueror.
I am fearfully and wonderfully made.
I am an overcomer.
I am able to do all things through Christ who strengthens me.

The people at Kadesh saw themselves as grasshoppers, but that's not how God saw them. Their self-concept caused them to count themselves out of what God had included them in. Chances are it's the same way with you.

- You look at your weakness. God looks at your strength.
- You look at what you can't do. God sees what you can do.
- You look at your sin. God looks at the cross that eclipses your sin.
- You look at your past. God looks at your future.
- You look at who's against you. God says, "If I'm for you then who can be against you?"

Do yourself a favor. Don't underestimate how the future of your life will be determined, in large part, by your own self-concept—by what you include yourself in or count yourself out of. Everyone who saw themselves like grasshoppers died in the wilderness. Not because that's what God wanted for them but because they were limited by their self-concept.

Joshua and Caleb serve as an example for all of us of what it means to be big on the inside and fight for your future. They never gave in to the grasshopper mentality. They saw themselves occupying the land of the giants. They focused their minds on the grapes and they fought for the future God had promised them. And they experienced the Promised Land!

Talk big to yourself. Talk faith to yourself. Remind yourself again and again, *The grapes are reachable, the giants defeatable, and I'm no grasshopper!*

1. Finish this statement, "The grapes are _____ _____, the giants _____, and I'm no _____."

2. What kind of spy would you have been to go scope out the Promised Land? Would you have focused on the size of the grapes? Or the size of the giants? Or how you thought you looked like a grasshopper in their eyes?

3. If the greatest enemy of your future is not what happens to you, what is it?

CHAPTER 20

MOVING BACK THE BOUNDARIES

Aboundary is something that we learn as a limit that we're not supposed to go beyond. There are lines we don't have permission to cross. There are places we are not authorized to go and buildings we're not supposed to go in. There are land boundaries and security boundaries. If you don't believe me, try breaching security the next time you're at the airport.

These are examples of external, social boundaries designed to keep us safe and respectful of other people's property as a society. But there is another kind of boundary, which is what this book has been about: the boundaries of our heart. Scripture tells us, "Keep your heart with all diligence, For out of it *spring* the issues of life" (Prov. 4:23 NKJV). There is a revelation in this verse that changed my life when I learned that the Hebrew word for issues is *towtsa'ah* (to-tsaw-aw), which is translated and defined in English as "boundaries." So you can think of it like this:

Above all else, guard your heart, for out of it comes the boundaries of your life. The writer is saying you should guard your heart because when the wrong stuff gets in your heart, it will put limits on your life where God hasn't put them.

We've all had that happen in one way or another, and the result is mental, spiritual, and emotional boundaries. Perhaps you've noticed that you can't seem to get past a certain point in your relationships. If so, you might have hit a relational boundary. If you've ever felt like you couldn't get past a certain point in your finances, you might have hit a financial boundary. If you've thought to yourself, *I want to grow spiritually, know God better, and read Scripture more,* but you stayed stuck in the same place, you might be hitting a spiritual boundary.

When you look back at times like that, chances are that in some of those cases you made an adjustment you needed to make or learned something you didn't know. And when you did, the relationship improved, the financial picture got better, or you experienced spiritual growth. In other words, you got bigger on the inside, which translated into progress in a specific area of your life. That's what happens when we have the right stuff in our hearts. We grow beyond the boundaries of our past and the limits of our history.

Financially: When we get the right stuff inside of us, our lives will prosper, increase, and grow. We will be rich in every way so that we can be generous on every occasion (see 2 Cor. 9:11).

Relationally: The extent of a person's friendship circle is also determined by the boundaries inside them. A person has friends because he is friendly (see Prov. 18:24).

Spiritually: Jesus was continually telling people to make room in their heart for the peace, joy, and abundant life of God. Making room for the Holy Spirit will push back the boundaries of worry and fear that try to take up all the space in your heart.

THE BOUNDARIES OF YOUR LIFE ARE NOT DETERMINED BY OTHER PEOPLE

I heard about a young guy at church who didn't like one of our young leaders. The guy he didn't like is one of the most likeable guys we've ever had on our team. I remember thinking, *What's not to like about him? If somebody doesn't like him, I don't have any chance of everybody liking me! Note to self, gonna give up on that right now!* Funny, but it's true. As you go through life it will become apparent that not everyone is going to like you. Some people are not going to see the potential in you. Some people are not going to cheer for you or go out of their way to help you. But relax, chill, and don't hold it against them. They don't determine the boundaries of your life.

Stay loose in your idea about what someone else can do or should do to open doors for you, phone a friend for you, or provide a platform to you. When you think that way, you set yourself up for unhealthy expectations of other people.

When you give others the power to determine the boundaries of your life, you become unreasonable and unfair toward them. If God uses them to open doors for you, be incredibly grateful, but don't assume that anyone owes you something. If you do, you'll set yourself up to be offended and then hold them responsible for your unmet expectations.

Remember, David's father didn't see his potential, David's brothers were envious of him, and King Saul was so jealous he tried to kill him—multiple times. In David's case, God used Jonathan (King Saul's son) to support him and brought people around him. David felt great gratitude toward them. But people didn't determine the boundaries of his life. And they don't determine the boundaries of your life.

THE BOUNDARIES OF YOUR LIFE ARE NOT DETERMINED BY CIRCUMSTANCES

The boundaries of our lives are not determined by the family we are born in or the neighborhood we grow up in. It's not about your family history, your economic status, or the color of your skin. When the heart is free to be big, it becomes a powerful and unstoppable force. There are many examples of people who grew up in the worst of circumstances and ended up with a life way beyond what circumstances had imposed on them.

Kyle Maynard is one of those people. He was born with a

disease, congenital amputation, which prevents the growth and development of limbs. Despite having arms that end at the elbows and legs that end near his knees, Kyle played youth football and wrestled in high school, winning thirty-six matches his senior year and placing twelfth in state. He is now an entrepreneur, a motivational speaker, and the best-selling author of *No Excuses*. He is the first quadruple amputee to climb (actually, bear crawl) Mount Kilimanjaro without the aid of prosthetics. He also climbed deadly Mount Aconcagua in Argentina, the highest peak in the western and southern hemispheres.[1]

I read a report on small businesses that said one in four new businesses close after one year, and half close after two years. Of the first-time entrepreneurs whose businesses closed quickly, the overwhelming majority—71 percent—didn't bother to try again. But the tenacious 29 percent who did were more likely to be successful the second, third, or even tenth time around. As crazy as it sounds, their success rate increased with their number of past failures.

Of the people who let failure get inside of them, 71 percent didn't try again. They hit a boundary and stayed within it. But the people who, in spite of a failed attempt, kept faith and optimism were able to use the bad experience as a benefit that eventually helped them succeed. These people had also hit a boundary but decided to move the boundary beyond the failure.[2]

Internal boundaries have nothing to do with circumstances or other people. Internal boundaries are not God's limits. An internal boundary has nothing to do with what's going on around you and everything to do with what's going on within you.

WHEN WE MOVE BACK THE INTERNAL BOUNDARIES, WE GET BIGGER ON THE INSIDE AND CREATE NEW REALITIES IN OUR FUTURE

This is why the Bible is so important to us. The Bible is God's word for our lives. When you read Scripture, talk Scripture, or memorize Bible verses, you bring the *dunamis*, the dynamite or dynamic power of God, into your heart.

Most of us have been on a road trip and seen places where rock walls or even mountains have been cut into with dynamite to allow a road or highway to go through. In the same way, God's word on the inside of us breaks down barriers, destroys walls, and moves mountains, creating paths for us into new territory, moving us beyond barriers, and expanding our lives into new places.

I know today that many of you have experienced exactly what I'm talking about—the power of God's word in your mind transforming you and giving you a Godly perspective over your circumstances, and the power of God's word in your confession that lifted heaviness off of you and put discouragement behind you.

There's a story in the Bible of a young man named Gideon who hated the circumstances he was in but was making no plans for anything better. He was doing what he had to do to survive but had no vision and no confidence for anything other than survival. That's when a messenger showed up with a word from God to Gideon. He said, "The LORD is with you, mighty warrior" (Judg. 6:12). "Really?" Gideon asked. "If God is with me, then why am I stuck here and why are my people in slavery?"

The messenger proceeded to let Gideon know that God was calling him to enlarge his thinking and elevate his attitude from a place of despair to a place of hope and confidence. God always begins his work in our lives by starting on the inside. This is what he was doing with Gideon. God wasn't speaking to who Gideon was; he was speaking to who Gideon was *meant to be*.

In the same way that my dad spoke to the mini-me and called out a bigger me, God spoke to the small, defeated Gideon and called him a warrior. God had bigger plans for Gideon, but he first needed Gideon to get bigger on the inside so he could do bigger things with his life.

Gideon argued with the messenger because he didn't realize that the limitations on his life were self-imposed. He was so self-absorbed and stuck in a victim mentality that he had put limits where God had provided wide-open spaces. His greatest challenge was not the enemy that held him and his people as slaves. The greatest enemy was the smallness inside of him.

Unless he overcame that, he would not experience the bigger future God had in mind for him and his people. When the messenger called him a mighty warrior, he was speaking God's word of affirmation and certainty about Gideon. He was calling him the person who God had equipped him to be: a warrior, a leader, and a liberator of his people.

Now Gideon had a decision to make. Was he going to believe what God said about him? Was he going to move the negativity out of his heart and replace it with God's word? God was calling Gideon to abandon the smallness, the lies, the discouragement, the defeat he was living in. To abandon his hopeless, helpless mindset and begin to see himself like God saw him.

As Gideon made the shift from an attitude of self-pity and helplessness, he started getting bigger on the inside. He became open to the possibilities that God was with him and that he was a mighty warrior. As his faith in God grew, he became more confident, and God was able to use him to lead his people from slavery into freedom.

It's a daunting thought to consider moments like this one in Gideon's life, when the future is determined by a single decision, a decision to stick with what I've believed to be true about myself or surrender my arguments and believe what God says about me.

DON'T COUNT YOURSELF OUT OF WHAT GOD HAS INCLUDED YOU IN

When you stop and think about it, the decisions like the one Gideon made not only change the trajectory of a person's life; they change the course of history. When a person sets aside a modest belief about themselves in exchange for a daring belief about their potential, it not only changes their life, it changes the future. It's as if something awakens inside of them, and they begin to walk in the divine destiny God had in mind for them all along.

> ## Don't count yourself out of what God has included you in.

Living in Seattle means seeing Starbucks stores almost as often as we see street corners. Starbucks chairman emeritus Howard Schultz wrote in his book *Pour Your Heart into It: How Starbucks Built a Company One Cup at a Time* about the big decision he made to leave the security net of his $75,000 salary to pursue his passion for all things coffee. *"This is my moment*, I thought. *If I don't seize the opportunity, if I don't step out of my comfort zone and risk it all, if I let too much time tick on, my moment will pass.* I knew that if I didn't take advantage of this opportunity, I would replay it in my mind for my whole life, wondering: *What if?"*[3] Five years later, Starbucks stock went public, and on June 26, 1992, it was the second most actively traded stock on the NASDAQ. There are now over twenty-nine thousand Starbucks stores around the world. The bigger the Starbucks story becomes, the more amazing it is that it can all be traced back to a single bold decision to make a move with no guarantee of the outcome.

It's more common than ever to overthink and underact. People talk themselves out of making a move that they want to make. They wonder things like, *What will people think? Am I ready for this? What if it doesn't work?* When people do that, they unknowingly miss out on opportunities and moments that God had included them in. It may sound a bit over the top, but consider this probability: At the end of your life your greatest regret won't be the things you did but wished you hadn't. Your greatest regret will be the things you didn't do but wish you had.

The Bible gives us examples of people who in moments of opportunity made bold moves that led them forward toward God's best for their life. When they made a move, walls came down, prisons opened, enemies were defeated, and battles were won.

It's no different for you. When you, by faith, push past hesitation to make a move, you engage possibilities that are otherwise impossible. Your experience changes, which means your story changes, which means your future changes.

Maybe you've never thought of it like this, but every emotion you feel has a specific physiology linked to it. Lifting your head can also lift your mood. Raising your hands in a sign of victory can raise the level of faith for victory. Putting your shoulders back can bring courage to your spirit. My point is that God has created us in such a way that even our most basic physical movements have a correlating effect on us. Now, imagine that in the form of intentional, consistent, unhindered movement in the direction of God's best for your life. Imagine that in the context of fighting for your future.

What's your next move?

As I've written this book, I've prayed you. Not by name, of course, but for you as I know you. The you that has something audacious, daring, and risky inside of you. The one who's been waiting in the window and longing to dance in the streets.

Borrowing some of the words from the apostle Paul's prayer in Ephesians 1:17–19:

I've prayed God would give you the Spirit of wisdom and revelation, that the eyes of your heart would be enlightened and that you would know God's incredible power for you when you believe.

That you will always...

Risk exposure
Abandon smallness
Push past criticism
Own your story
Fight for your future

Study Questions

1. Where do the boundaries of your life come from? How would you describe internal boundaries?
2. How can you move back the self-imposed boundaries of your life? What happens when you do?

3. What are some areas that you have been counting yourself out of where God has wanted to include you?
4. What does vulnerability mean to you now? How has it changed as you've read this book?
5. What are three things you can apply to your life in the next three weeks that you have learned reading this book?

NOTES

I. RISK EXPOSURE

Chapter 2. The Risk of Exposure

1 Paul Harris, "Focus: How Condoleezza Rice Became the Most Powerful Woman in the World," *The Guardian*, January 16, 2005.

2 Steven Curtis Chapman, "The Great Adventure," Sparrow, Phil Naish, June 1992.

3 Lee Ann Womack et al., "I Hope You Dance," MCA Nashville, Mark Wright, September 1999.

Chapter 3. Playing It Safe Is Dangerous

1 "William Carey," *Christian History | Learn the History of Christianity and the Church*, Christian History, February 18, 2016.

Chapter 4. Comfort Is Way Overrated

1   Mike Mitchell, director, *The Lego Movie 2: The Second Part*, Warner Animation Group, Warner Bros. Pictures, 2019.

2   "Roosevelt's 'The Man in the Arena,'" *Mental Floss*, April 23, 2015.

II. ABANDON SMALLNESS

Chapter 5. Growing Bigger on the Inside

1   Marianne Williamson, *A Return to Love: Reflections on the Principles of "A Course in Miracles"* (New York: HarperCollins, 1992).

Chapter 6. Getting Beyond the Fear Fence

1   Margie Warrell, "Do You Overestimate Risk and Underestimate Yourself?" *Forbes*, April 17, 2015.

2   Kevin Gerald, *Good Things: Seeing Your Life Through the Lens of God's Favor* (Colorado Springs: WaterBrook Press, 2015), p. 19.

Chapter 7. Sand and Stars

1   Cat Clifford, "How Charity: Water's Founder Went from Hard-Partying NYC Club Promoter to Helping 8 Million People around the World," CNBC, March 22, 2018.

Chapter 8. Think 3

1   Julie Bort, "This 9-Year-Old Girl Just Got a Shout Out by Apple CEO Tim Cook," *Business Insider*, June 13, 2016.

III. PUSH PAST CRITICISM

Chapter 11. Filters

1   Kevin Gerald, *Mind Monsters: Conquering Fear, Worry, Guilt, and Other Negative Thoughts That Work against You* (Lake Mary, FL: Charisma House, 2012).

Chapter 12. Don't Come Down

1   Josh Berhow, "All the Times Writers (Including Our Own), Analysts, and Pros Were Wrong about Woods," Golf.com, September 23, 2018.

IV. OWN YOUR STORY

Chapter 14. Unoffendable

1   Brett Ratner, director, *The Family Man*, Universal Pictures, 2000.

V. FIGHT FOR YOUR FUTURE

Chapter 17. Being Your Best in the Stress

1   Bill Gates, "This Ingenious Machine Turns Feces into Drinking Water," Gatesnotes.com, January 5, 2015.

Chapter 19. Grapes, Giants, and Grasshoppers

1   Mark Burnett, *Jump In! Even If You Don't Know How to Swim* (New York: Ballantine Books, 2005).

Chapter 20. Moving Back the Boundaries

1   "Entrepreneur + Athlete + Speaker," Kyle-Maynard.com, http:// kyle-maynard.com/about-kyle.
2   Allison Schrager, "Failed Entrepreneurs Find More Success the Second Time," *Bloomberg*, July 28, 2014.
3   Howard Schultz and Dori Jones Yang, *Pour Your Heart Into It: How Starbucks Built a Company One Cup at a Time* (New York: Hachette, 2014).

ACKNOWLEDGMENTS

The writing of this book was transformative and at the same time difficult. For me to write on this topic seemed presumptuous on my part. Mainly, because I'm not even close to being an expert on the topic. Which is one of several reasons why I could not have completed this book without the help and support of a number of important people in my life.

Thanks first to Sheila, my wife and life partner for forty-one years. Sheila, you have been an inspiring force in my life. Your belief in me gives me confidence and courage to step out and commit myself to doing what is in my heart to do.

Thank you to my kids, my daughter Jodi and her husband Ryan. Jodi for the critique, the suggestions, the readiness to always help me get unstuck. Ryan, for believing in and encouraging me. The understanding and grace the two of you show me means a lot and makes the writing more rewarding.

Thank you, Jen, for managing me through this project and keeping all of us on track and headed in the right direction.

Thank you to Jessica. I'm grateful for you, the possibilities you saw, and the value you placed on this message. Without you this book would not have happened.

Thank you to my publisher, FaithWords and Hatchette Book Group, for the opportunity.

Thank you, editors Keren and Virginia. To Keren for the key part you played beginning in the early stages of this process and your expertise throughout. To Virginia for coming alongside, considering us, prompting us, and getting us to the finish line.

To all of the home team, the people who I do life and ministry with on a weekly basis, it's an honor to serve with you on behalf of heaven. Thank you for being family to me. Thank you for your prayers, your words of affirmation, and for being a constant source of inspiration on this book and beyond. It's a privilege to be your pastor.

ABOUT THE AUTHOR

Whether speaking on a platform or writing his next book, Kevin Gerald encourages others to move life forward using practical biblical principles. Kevin is a recognized, sought-after communicator, speaking internationally at events and conferences. He also provides leadership development for church teams and leaders through an organization known as Team Church. Kevin founded and currently pastors Champions Centre, which is one of the largest nondenominational churches in the Northwest. When not co-pastoring with his wife, Sheila, he enjoys sports, being a papa, and exploring the great outdoors. You can learn more about him at http://kevingerald.com.

If you enjoyed *Naked and Unafraid*, equip yourself with additional resources at www.nakedandunafraidbook.com.

Connect with Kevin Gerald:
Facebook: www.facebook.com/kevingeraldcommunications